CW01095435

It's All About the Honey

It's All About the Honey

From Striving to Sweet Presence

A testimony and revelations from
Jesus Christ
by
Jacqueline Taylor

Edited: Julie Brown
Cover design:Jacqueline Taylor and Janegibbscreative
Cover artwork: Olga Koelsh from Designbundles
Publisher: Jane Gibbs KDP Publishing Services

Dedication

To my husband, Rod, who has walked every part of this journey with me, supports me every step of the way, and has the courage to grow in depth with Jesus as we go.

I deeply appreciate the time alone you have given me, not only for this project, but for the space I need when seeking Jesus' heart.

And for being the voice of reason when my emotions wanted to rule.

I love you man.

Acknowledgements

It is with the deepest gratitude in my heart that I acknowledge Julie Brown for the input she has had in producing this book you now hold. Her constant encouragement in The Proverbs 31 Movement Book Coaching Journey, was honest, authentic, and loving. My life will never be the same for meeting this precious woman. She is a true Lover of Jesus, pure in heart and intention.

I would also like to give a shout out to the beautiful group of people I am proud to call Sisters in Christ who were part of my book writing journey with Julie. Jennifer De Moss, a constant support and friend, Marlene Bond, whom it was an absolute pleasure to spend time with in New Zealand, and who also contributed to the editing process. Jenny Watson, whom I am so grateful to for taking the time to read my book before publishing, Barbara McNeice, whom I look forward to meeting with all my heart.

I sincerely look forward to reading and gleaning from all of YOUR books and experiences you are willing to share from the heart of Jesus.

Thank you to Joanne Starke and Tracy Corbin for taking the time to read and give honest input when the manuscript was in it's skeleton form.

Amy Webb. In the process of this unfolding journey, your patience with me in regards to 'The Bee' and your generosity in sharing your artwork, has blessed me no end. I hope I do her justice with her use in future books and journals.

To Liz Wright for bringing me from 'there,' to 'here.' Words cannot express.

Endorsements

"Jacqueline's first book, 'It's All About the Honey' touched my life so deeply, right in the heart of my heart. There is a life-giving flow, like a sparkling stream of refreshing waters to revive even the most weary traveller and that flow is the testimony of Jacqueline's deep, experiential relationship with Jesus. Authentic and honest, parts of this book are so powerful that you will begin to find yourself moving, supernaturally, out of a well worn pathway of 'striving', into the hope of 'the sweet honey of His Presence' that Jacqueline so beautifully describes. No matter what your relationship with Jesus has been, this book will draw you into a realm where you begin to long for more of the One that loves you, a daily experience where you enter into Rest and drink deeply of Him. Jacqueline's experience can be yours too. This book is like the most beautiful fruit, hanging from the Vine that is Him. Well done Jacqueline.. I love it.."

Julie H Brown,
Author & Founder of The Proverbs 31 Movement

"In her first book *'Its All About the Honey - From Striving to Sweet Presence'*, Jacqueline shares nuggets from her own personal experience that will help the reader to explore, engage with and encounter the tenderness and wonder of the Spirit of God. The poetic overflow and transparency in this publication will draw you deeply to renewed pursuit of the Lover of your soul. Prepare to be awakened to fresh revelation and adventures in the secret place of His Presence."

Jenny Watson
Apostolic Leader, Kingdom Advance Network, UK
Author: Determine Your Direction
jenwatson.co.uk

"This book will change you. It contains truths only a heart that has discovered the deeper life of true union with Jesus can know. These truths are an invitation for us to live immersed in Gods presence. To rest in the wisdom and security of His ways as we lose our life to find Him through the doorway of surrender.

As you read you will recognise some of your own story as Jacqueline authentically shares hers. You will find yourself untangling from exhausting religious striving and becoming free to simply enjoy Jesus as you enter into the deeper life Jacqueline has so clearly experienced. The life we are all invited to enjoy."

Liz Wright,
Founder of The International Mentoring Community
International Best Selling Author.
Host of Live Your Best Life

"I commend this book to anyone struggling with serving outside their calling. The author, Jacqueline, shares her own experience of serving because there was a need, then finding freedom to serve within her calling, and the move of the Holy Spirit in her life as a result. I hope you enjoy reading this book, and that it blesses you as you seek The Lord on its application for your life. "

Pastor Juan Lorca
One Direction Church Fellowship
Bunbury, Western Australia

"Jacqueline's first book, 'It's All About the Honey' is a beautiful personal account of her journey from religion, striving and works, to the rising of a new well spring within her, when she least expected it, that would bring her into a new and marvellous encounter with her lover and beloved, as she learns to do the bridal dance of her life! Not only do I love the way this book depicts some of the age-old truths from the books of Apostle Paul, e.g., our incapacity to do anything of ourselves, grace from start to finish, our new life in Christ, our freedom, heirship, inheritance and authority in Christ too, is encapsulated beautifully, throughout the book.

This book however, is not a book of just facts and knowledge, there is a strong air of the supernatural intertwined in the pages of this book, from start to finish. Evident is the pure breath of Holy Spirit, the sweet-smelling fragrance of Jesus Christ and the hot fire of the Father's heart for his beloveds! It will draw you into a new and fresh encounter with the King of Kings and may even carry you away into raptures and visions. I believe it has the capacity too, to activate, signs, wonders and miracles. In this book, we are going over to the other side. Jesus, through Jaqueline's account, is taking us there! The best wine, until last! I love it!"

Pastor Yvonne Hale
The Ark, Perth.
LFCC Belfast Prophetic Centre

Contents

Foreword

I have a feeling that upon reading Jacqueline's powerful testimony, a multitude of those of us who relate to working hard proving our worth to Jesus, will emerge like little animals that burrow underground. (In the USA we have groundhogs and moles, I have no idea what might crawl underground in Australia or anywhere else in the world.)

For years we buried ourselves and dug furiously in the hard ground with various motives to establish the ministries and platforms of others, while competing for our own voices to be heard. We longed to see daylight and knew the existence of it was just overhead. Simply peeking out of our burrows rewarded us with burning eyes and an exaggerated fear of freedom when seeing the expanse of what was truly available.

The dilemma before us was that to live above ground in the light meant that we would have to stop the scratching, the crawling, the endless working forward in our own energy which literally drove us in circles. Religion does not want us to see light, ever, no matter how good we are at proving ourselves.

Jacqueline tenderly yet confidently brings us to the remedy, which is to say that there is no remedy, only REST in our Beloved.

Jacqueline and I met at the start of Liz Wright's International Mentoring Community in 2020, coming from similar places of a sort of forced invitation from Jesus into rest. Submitting to physical rest was not an option, but surrender to the deep change that Jesus was inviting us to, was. I believe this book is the fruit of Jacqueline's journey of loving and willing surrender to Jesus, and the truth she has learned in this place is profound. It is truth that cannot be learned or carried any other way than through surrender.

As I read Jacqueline's book, I often had to stop and let Jesus' words to her unwind my own heart, receiving freedom from the beliefs that led me underground in the first place. I encourage you to do the same; read this book slowly and intentionally, taking time to stop where Holy Spirit lingers.

The IMC is an environment absent of competition or hierarchy, and full of unconditional love and honor.

We have all grown in our capacity to receive from Jesus solely because that's what He created us for. It has also been a healthy place for friendships to grow, and getting to know Jacqueline has been one of my most special treasures from being in the IMC. If you are tired of being driven by religion's demands and are longing for true connection with Jesus, you will find a beautiful path to such a place here through Jacqueline's story.

Jennifer DeMoss
Author and Creative.
A Community of Esthers: Confident, Favored, Revealed.

Introduction

I took a detour, purposely, because of a word of knowledge my husband gave me, where Holy Spirit spoke telling him I needed to go a long way around to my destination. Thinking this was to avoid an accident, or road-work delay, I did as per the instruction.

I had left my home, in Capel, Western Australia, and was on my way to my prayer house, in Narrogin. The detour took me through country I hadn't travelled before, and Google maps cut out half way down the gravel road I was travelling on, but I wasn't aware of this. When I exited onto the main road again, I was still some distance from where I was heading and a fair bit south of my intended destination.

On this 'detour' Holy Spirit descended into my car, covering me in the sweet honey of His presence, pouring revelation into me, through the not unhappy circumstance I was in. I was filled with such peace, and love, I had to stop at one point to have a little cry.

What He was showing me, apart from the obvious of trusting Him to lead, was that He was extending my boundaries, and taking me to places I hadn't been before.

He spoke through the fields around me, telling me He had already equipped me for the Harvest (there were acres and acres of wheat fields surrounding me), and there wasn't anything in me that needed to be burnt up by fire, at this stage. (I saw a field of dry stubble). The fiery refining process was being exchanged for peace. Liquid gold anointing was flowing in me and through me. The winter had passed.

I then had a vision of Jesus handing me this book I am writing now, with a red heart made of velvet on top of it, and a large old-fashioned key. It was as if the book was finished with His heart, and the words within are the key to the door of what was written in our blueprints thousands of years ago. I peacefully travelled this detour surrounded in Him, and unhindered by the restraints of time.

Unhindered by the restraints of time…

My life is busy (I know you can relate). So, to be unhindered by time is a massive shift. Over the following days, imprinted in my spirit man, was the need to breathe, go slow, and just do what I felt like doing. Which was just to breathe and go slow. Totally foreign to me at the time, but a way of living that I longed for.

I was then tested in the ability to go slow in my normal everyday life on the day I was due to return to Capel.

My son phoned me, saying, "Lovely day for a picnic with the kids Mum. Come on." My time-driven old thought patterns pushed in with anxiety. I asked him to give me 10 minutes to respond (there is a key for you), and hung up. This trip to see my family would take me 45 minutes further away from my Capel home, meaning a 3-hour trip at the end of the day.

Here is the miracle. Holy Spirit cut through that anxiety, with 'Go Slow. Go. Enjoy. And Go Slow.' So instead of rushing around like a blue bottomed fly, I finished doing what I was doing and headed off.

As I drove through the flowered paddocks in the country, once again Holy Spirit descended into the car. He came with a steel plate that was slotted between my old way of moving, and this new way. I pulled to the side of the road again to absorb what He was imparting to me.

Even if I have things to do, and places to be…

GO SLOW AND IN PEACE

He wasn't taking away the tasks, or the business I needed to run, or the family I needed to tend to, or the people on my path who needed a touch from Him.

He was rearranging my thinking so I could do all that…

WITHOUT ANXIETY AND STRESS

I can choose to walk at a slower pace with the same amount of activity!!!

And so, I enjoyed the picnic, my son, my daughter-in-law, and my 4 little granddaughters, and drove home in another cloud of life-giving peace.

Then my week turned to custard, and I had to work 6 days out of the coming 7, just to test out my new mind set! How did I go?

 God re-arranged the whole week. I surrendered, made a decision to walk in the way that had just been imparted to me, travelled 3 hours to a meeting, and in that meeting, my precious son re-dedicated himself to The Lord.

All of this is important for me to say, before I lead into anything else, as this is the outcome of laying down my life in surrender to **His** ways.

As I surrendered to His heart, and His thinking, I came to a place of knowing that I know, that He lives in me and there is no need for me to strive and try anymore.

Oh, what a glorious shift from previous years of performance-based movement.

There are still things that need to change, and wrong beliefs that need shifting, but this book is evidence of a miracle working Holy Spirit, where, with His help, and my surrender, I will bare my all, and hopefully encourage someone to get off the hamster wheel of religious activity, and into the deep, secret place with Christ, to be changed forever, as I have been.

> "…the bondage of your barren winter has ended, and the season of hiding is over and gone… Can you not discern this new day of destiny breaking forth around you?…There is change in the air."
>
> Song of Songs 2:11, 13 (TPT)

Maybe you have a detour going on in your life right now, that you don't quite understand?

In my experience of the grace and kindness of God, detours always lead back to Him having His way. Usually in unexpected, surprising sorts of ways.

As you surrender to a place of rest, relaxing into Jesus heart, you will begin to enjoy the journey and what is happening around and within yourself, on the way to your destination.

One

A Vision –
Honey from the Rock

I had a vision of standing at a rock. It was sitting between my soul (mind, will and emotions) and a rich deep pool of golden, sweet liquid. I had been drilling at the rock myself with a small hand-held drill, without barely making a mark. Jesus was standing next to me. He ushered in a helper who had been standing behind us. This helper had a jack hammer. The jack hammer hit the rock, and I suddenly became aware that if Jesus would only but touch this rock, it would split apart. I didn't want to tell him what to do, or guide my imagination in a way that was out of His will, but I looked at Him in this vision and He touched it.

The vision of me drilling, and then the jack hammer coming in next was to prepare my mind for what would happen when the golden liquid began to flow. It would flood. Flood everywhere. Take over the world, we would all be swimming in it, carried along with it.

As this sweet honey gushed over the rock that had split, it covered the rock like an ocean, and I was carried along. I was then drawn back in the spirit, and I saw this gold veil of glory cover the Earth, East to West first, then North to South. I was in it, watching it, part of it, directing it, with Holy Spirit, governing from a distance in worship and dance. It was intense and powerful and so beautiful. I asked Jesus what it was - what was this honey, this glory - how did it manifest between people, and in the Earth right now?

He said:

"Kindness, Love, Peace. This sweet glory manifests by those who are walking with me, being carriers of sweetness in chaos. It is my majesty and strength, shining through my shining ones.

Tap into the vision of being a carrier of sweetness, without striving. Have faith that you carry me, and it is I, through you, who dispenses strength, peace, joy, comfort, healing, breakthrough. Be a partaker of this understanding – eat of it. Taste and see my goodness in the land of the living.

I long to use you, and for you to be unhindered by the ceiling of false humility.

Shine brightly – My Glory rises upon you. Shine and don't hold back.

Encourage others to shine. See through My eyes, those

around you who are seeking me. Encourage them to also look with my eyes.

Be a carrier of this sweet vision and a dispenser of it.

Remember this, and when you feel striving ebbing in again, come back into me, and pick up the sweet honey of presence and fruits of My Spirit, to again dispense the multi-layered dimensions of glory throughout, and over the world.

Your confidence allows grace and majesty to manifest. Confidence in me and who I am in you. Confidence in what you know of who you are to me."

And this was the end of the vision. The powerful scripture in 2 Timothy came immediately to mind:

"The saying is trustworthy, for If we have died with Him, we will also live with Him; If we endure, we will also reign with Him."

2 Timothy 2:11-13 (ESV)

This is not some distant reality which we aspire to. This is how we are to walk now on this Earth, with the authority given to Adam, taken by the devil, and given back through the appropriated Blood of Jesus. Our destiny is to walk in the esteemed position as a Bride, co-reigning with Christ, our Lord and Saviour:

"When I look at you, I see how you have taken my fruit and tasted my word. Your life has become clean and pure, like a lamb washed and newly shorn…

When I look at you, I see your inner strength, so stately

and strong. You are as secure as David's fortress…

Your pure faith and love rest over your heart as you nurture those who are yet infants.

Now you are ready, My Bride, to come with me as we climb the highest peaks together. Come with me through the archway of trust. We will look down from the crest of the glistening mounts and from the summit of our sublime sanctuary. Together we will wage war in the lion's den and the leopard's lair as they watch nightly for their prey."

Songs of Songs 4:2,4,5,8 (TPT)

Two

Come to My Shoulder

My heart's desire has always been to draw all that I see in the Spirit.

I practice this now, but currently my drawing and painting is not fit for public consumption. If I could, I would fill reams of paper with colour and glory that surpasses the imagination.

When I have entered into rest with Holy Spirit, choosing to sink into Christ in me, my imagination travels to places of revelation in picture form. I have visions. But, because I am not an artist, yet, I write.

The words in poetry in this book stem from visions I have had. This seems to be the best way to describe where I have been, what I have seen, and the revelations that come from the realm of God's Kingdom. In poetry I attempt to convey the heart of Jesus, and the insight of Holy Spirit in a simple form. It is, after all, a simple gospel: Christ within, separation denied, union with our Creator, God Divine.

The poetry that follows is prophetic, spoken to my heart by Holy Spirit:

'Come to My Shoulder' – A Poem Spoken by Jesus

"So, come to my shoulder and listen awhile, as I lay down the plan, watch and see.

Come to my shoulder and watch as I play, as I dance and create what you'll be.

Watch me, my daughter, as I mould and I sculpt. As I shave and I squeeze and I shape.

Watch as I speak over you all my love, and into you, all my plans make.

You've been on the inside, looking only from pain, where the pressure seems hard to bear.

But I want you to look from the place where I sit. I want you to come, meet me there.

The years you saw trouble, and trying and strife, I had you in the palm of my hand.

The years you screamed, in white noise - trying - I was spinning you into my plan.

I was loving you as my table it turned, to you it was seasons, and years.

Sometimes you thought I was finished, but not I,

I continued to squeeze and you teared.

It's not cruelty, or anger, or punishment I bring. It's a shaping of your destiny.

It's not because you are not worthy right now. You are all you're created to be.

You cannot see it from where you stand now, so come up – up higher and look!

You need my perspective to see what I'm doing.

Then you'll know how to read your own book.

Your thinking is tainted from being in this world. It's that which I scrape away.

I'm taking you through circumstance so you can see, what needs to go, what needs to stay.

My intention is only great love and great joy. Come see all I created you to be.

A vessel of pure intention and trust. Pure motives that have set you free.

I called you to lay down all I had given, the striving, the being ruled by fear.

Ego and pride had blinded your eyes, and death was the way down from there.

But now come and look, as I've cleared your eyes, given clear vision and truth.

Of my holy love, of our union of trust. A rising up, drawing forth, bringing through.

You are my love, my fair one. Rise up in life and be strong.

Come up the stair, through the archway of trust, breathe in the place you belong.

Yes, my child, dance with me. It Is Finished, and that you can see.

We are one, you and I, and I want to show you – what happens when you're truly free..."

Our perspective is so often tainted by what we see with our natural eyes, but as this poem suggests, there is a call to a higher place, an intimate place, where He will reveal the nature of our walk. It is God's will and desire that we understand His ways, and that we have an expectation to hear His voice.

He is speaking all the time, and His voice uniquely caters to our way of hearing. Quiet your glorious soul. Love your busy brain, honour your emotions. But put them in their rightful place, which is under the governance of your Spirit.

Holy Spirit will speak to you Spirit to spirit, not Spirit to brain. You have been awakened, and you can hear. It is not just for the prophets and those who have words of wisdom and knowledge to hear the voice of God. We have all received of the same Spirit, and now are coming into a revelation of our oneness with Him. We ALL hear. We are ALL being drawn into a higher, deeper walk with Him.

So come to His shoulder and listen. Let Him reveal His heart, His nature, and His purpose to you.

Three

Living in Union with Christ

"There is a divine mystery – a secret surprise that has been concealed from the world for generations, but now it's being revealed, unfolded and manifested for every holy believer to experience. Living within you is the Christ who floods you with the expectation of glory! This mystery of Christ, embedded within us, becomes a heavenly treasure chest of hope filled with the riches of glory for his people, and God wants everyone to know it!"

Colossians 1:26-27 (TPT)

CHRIST IN ME. IN ME...

I love this Colossians scripture. The secret surprise now being revealed is Christ living in you the hope of glory!!!! Holy, holy God!!! Our eyes are being opened to this great mystery, the greatest revelation ever known to man – the glory of God dwelling on the inside of man.

It takes a whole lot of dismantling of the old ways to truly comprehend, live and walk in this revelation, but the following scripture in Acts clearly states that it is in Him and through Him we live and move and have our being:

Christ and Him glorified in and through you. He made from one man every nation of mankind to live on the face of the earth, having determined their appointed times, and the boundaries of their lands and territories. (Taken from Acts 17)

"This was so that they would seek God, if perhaps they might grasp for Him and find Him, though He is not far from each one of us. For in Him we live and move and exist (that is, in Him we actually have our being)."

Acts 17:27-28 (AMP)

I heard the Lord say:

"The call you hear to come up here, come up here, is a call to come in, come in. Come INTO ME, where you belong, where you were destined to be, and where I called you to from the beginning of ages. I called you to me, and I sent Holy Spirit to dwell INSIDE of you. YOU are a temple of Holy Spirit. I AM IN YOU. YOU ARE IN ME."

"The glory that you have given me I have given to them, that they may be one even as we are one, I in them and you in me, that they may become perfectly one, so that the world may know that you sent me and loved them even as you loved me. I have made known to them your name, and I will continue to make it known, that the love with which you have loved me may be in them, and I in them."

John 17:22,26 (ESV)

The sweet revelation honey flowing from the throne of God is that of our **union with Christ**. It is Holy Spirit's wisdom, revelation, healing and restoration flowing, as you enter into the promised land.

Our oneness with Him which has perhaps been smothered in works, performance, and busy-ness in His name, is now being illuminated by the power of His Spirit.

Our ways of speaking, and communicating with one another, have clouded the mystery of our union with Christ. The rhetoric of the past is now being dissolved around us.

GOD is having His perfect way, as men and women who now seek after the pure heart of God are rising up in strength and wisdom, to share revelations of truth, gained through the study of the Hebrew, Aramaic and Greek languages.

Christ is also revealing Himself and His resurrection power by taking us into depths of encounters with Him, bringing revelation of the truth through the word like we have never experienced before.

"I will lead the blind by ways they have not known, along unfamiliar paths I will guide them; I will turn darkness into light before them, and make the rough places smooth. These are the things I will do. I will not forsake them."

"The mature children of God are those who are moved by the impulses of the Holy Spirit. And you did not receive the "spirit of religious duty" leading you back into the fear of never being good enough. But you have received the "spirit of full acceptance," enfolding you into the family of God."

Romans 8:14 (TPT)

It is time to release the old and step into the fullness of the mystery of Christ and our union with the Godhead. We are His glorious Bride.

It has taken me many years to understand that being His Bride requires intimacy at a level I didn't even know existed. The keys are being given to us now, and the doors are being opened for this revelation to pour out on those who are willing to surrender and yield to oneness.

Are you ready to give it all up for Jesus?

Are you hungering for something, yet don't know what that something actually is?

I was too and now I have found it.

It is Intimacy.

It is sweet, heart connection in the depths of my soul, being satisfied with the marrow and fatness of his Presence.

This is where a table is laid before you in the presence of your enemies, where you drink with deep thirst-quenching gulps from the wells of salvation.

I will take you now on the journey I have travelled, out of the desolate land of Egyptian bondage, into the land flowing with milk and honey. My hope is that as you travel the journey with me, you also will be drawn out of the works you have been entangled in, entering into the greatest depths of intimacy you have ever known.

Four

A Vision - Keys

I had a vision, before I was shifted from religion to relationship, of thousands of keys:

I was standing on a big pile of keys, throwing them out to people by the handful. Becoming frustrated, I thought, "there has to be a better way!" Then a plane came to a halt above me, and sucked me up into its belly, along with all the keys. We flew over crowds of people dispersing keys from the belly of the plane. I was excited about this destiny I saw before me.

I then had a second vision a couple of years later:

This vision was of Jesus standing near me, as I lay sunburnt and exhausted, in a row boat on the ocean. He asked me to give him back all the keys. I was happy in an angry kind of way to do that. Bitter and despondent, I threw keys at Him…

This sounds like I lacked a fear of The Lord, but the honest truth was I was angry, tired, hurt and broken. Angry with God, with people and with my life. I was full of pain in my body, from working in a physically demanding job, resentful, carrying self-pity and blame. Worst of all I was sick of heart at lost hopes and dead dreams.

 When I had first become a Christian, I was full of life and joy. As I entered into the life of church and service, this became my way of 'being a Christian': Working hard, being where I should at the right time, going to the meetings etc. It was my life, AND I LOVED IT. I thought it was all there was to being a Christian. And yet, I had a hole on the inside of me, a hunger never quite satisfied. I thought that was because I needed to learn something else. Know more, get more knowledge, more deliverance, serve in a greater way.

I had been in this striving way of thinking and operating for a long time. But The Lord of Glory, and my Sovereign King was about to shift me in a way only He can.

My second vision continued…

I was left stranded in a row boat, holding one key. Jesus held out His hand for the last one. A little surprised that I wanted to hold onto it, I reluctantly let it go. I lay down in the scorching sun, in the bottom of the little boat, exhausted, hurting and broken.

Suddenly a big wave came, my boat turned into a surfboard, and I was riding a great big wave, with no supports, no anchor, no oars, totally dependent on the wave, taken wherever that wave wanted to go, and hanging on for dear life, as I had no control.

I had been moving in my own strength, now it was time to ride the wave of The Spirit. Totally out of control, in Him.

Of course, the wave didn't manifest overnight. In fact, it took another 4 years before I began to sense a movement in the depths of the waters, but in the handing back of the keys, I was laying down in surrender. I must say it was out of exhaustion, and not obedience, but the end result was the same. I was surrendering.

It took this exhausted state for Jesus to get me right where He wanted me. In His hands, where I had to trust fully in Him. He had a plan for me, and He has a plan for you too.

When Jesus asked me to hand Him back the keys, he wasn't angry with me. I had done the best I could with all I knew, though moving out of my own strength. It was time for me to let go of control, and let Him show me the way forward.

Quite a number of years later, some of the master keys were given back to me. I then had a deeper understanding of their significance, and moreover, a deeper sense of their holiness.

So, I surrendered. My encouragement to you, is that you also surrender. But do so with great hope for your future.

Jesus has not finished with you, even though the process feels like death. It is. It is death to yourself. But what rises up – what is resurrected when you have died, is far beyond anything you can ask or think.

The Lord is moving sovereignly now. He is moving quickly. If you are one who is being moved out of a works mentality, despondent in lost dreams and hope deferred, be still. Your salvation is nigh unto thee.

There are times where your dreams need to be laid down, and you yield. You maybe feeling destitute, without direction, or movement, or purpose, but my friend, be still. Those that wait upon The Lord Shall renew their strength. (Isaiah 40)

I love the Hebrew word for *'wait'* in Isaiah 40:31 - qavah – it brings a picture of 'binding together, by twisting.' So, as you wait upon The Lord, sitting, yielding, resting, meditating on His Word, you are binding yourself together with Him. You are becoming one with Him as He broods over you to bring about the plans and purposes of Himself within you.

In this place, His love teaches a new way of life, where we carry the joy and peace of our Saviour, as we walk fully partaking of, and distributing the fruits of the Spirit.

It is not by might or power, in which some of us have walked up until now, but by the Spirit of The Lord. Walking in this intimacy causes the striving to cease, and allows Him to move freely. A flow begins to happen as we trust Him to have His way, in our homes, in the buildings of our fellowships, in the streets. We don't need to worry about the programs anymore, as He is about to pour out His Spirit on all flesh, and we get to be witnesses.

Revelation as sweet as honeycomb is developing richly in your innermost being, where Jesus is hungering for you, more than you hunger for Him.

He is pouring out His Spirit, and His plans are coming to pass now, that no eye has seen and no ear has heard - yet He is revealing it to His sons by His Spirit.

"Things never discovered or heard of before, things beyond our ability to imagine – these are the many things God has in store for all his lovers. But God now unveils these profound realities to us by the Spirit. Yes, he has revealed to us His inmost heart and deepest mysteries through the Holy Spirit, who constantly explores all things."

1 Corinthians 2:9-10 (TPT)

Five

Acts of Service – From Love

Doing acts of service and ministry out of a need for acceptance and recognition is no longer a mode of operation, as Jesus strips away that which is no longer necessary. He releases us from false burdens, wrong mindsets, and unfulfilling activities, shifting us into the reality of being His son and His Bride.

This is not to say that acts of service and ministry are being done away with, but they are being moved into second position, behind the love relationship between us and our Saviour. We are returning to our first love.

When our calling and destiny is in right alignment, coming under the headship of Christ, and not from human agenda and motive, acts of service and ministry are then walked in with a greater weight of authority. A depth of power is released like never before.

Our Father's greatest desire is that we walk in the

fullness of all He has called us to be. He has begun an equipping that is coming from His heart, surpassing all the works and strivings of man.

Take a moment here, to ask Holy Spirit, are there areas I am walking in that are not conducive with this season in my life?

Are there dreams, ideals, ways of walking with Christ that I need to let go of, to make room for the new places He is taking me?

As we join together in union with Christ - which leads us into union with our brothers and sisters in Christ - the fullness of His will is revealed.

In the past, we have had this the wrong way around. *Trying* to love, to show His love, to be in His love - instead of *allowing His love* to produce love in and through us, towards others.

When you sink into His presence and gaze upon Love, you become what you look at. Loving your enemy is no longer something you need to think about. Jesus is love, and love flows forth from your inner man, without striving, trying or thought. You become Love, as He is Love.

Honey

I am an apiarist. I love bees and Jesus has revealed

Himself to me in visions, using honey as a very present and real picture for me.

A few months back, one of the frames in my hive needed replacing. It was full of honey. I took this frame to my kitchen, and, absolutely undone and weeping at the profound nature of what was happening, began to cut the dripping honeycomb up. What was being intensely pressed into my spirit was how sweet it is to walk in the heart of Jesus. His love was overtaking me, and nothing else mattered in the world except for standing in His presence right there.

I was, for a long moment, sobbing, soaking in the reality of His love, being overcome and saturated within by the union of our being, as honey dripped from my hands. It was a day I will never forget.

I didn't need to strive or work for this honey. I just had to be there. I became a partaker of what is the natural wonder of honey. Gods' creation had done the work, and I was basking in the golden glory. How sweet is the Fathers' love for us!

Each one of us is called into this kind of union with Him, drawn by His Spirit, into His presence. From this place of true connection with Jesus, you will know what you are called to and your ministry will reach its fulfillment. For your heart to be filled with a desire to do His will, and run your race with purpose, touches His heart.

You are moving Him in your passion and excitement to

be a part of the biggest story the world has been waiting for. You also move Him with your strategizing and planning.

Knowing your destiny is important to God. But knowing who you are in Him, how much you are loved, treasured and set apart, just because you are *you*, and have been chosen by Him, and accepted Him, is far more important to the heart of God, than what you do.

This is the honey. This is the food you are hungering after. This is the sweetness that sustains your soul.

You are loved.

You are treasured.

You don't have to perform.

You are accepted as you are.

Joy is yours.

Peace is yours.

Salvation, forgiveness, redemption…all yours.

You do not need to strive for perfection before you are accepted.

YOU ALREADY ARE ACCEPTED.

Six

The Better Portion

In Luke 10: 38-42, Martha thought it was more important to make Jesus lunch. This was her way, and she had always been like that. A server.

Her eyes were not yet open to the fact that if she sat still, at Jesus' feet, her Spirit would be awakened and ignited by passion, her soul washed, and her heart filled with all fullness. Her toil would become joyful, not a burden, her works a service of love, not a necessity.

Mary chose the better portion. Her adoration and sitting at His feet were esteemed by Jesus as the right thing to do.

Serving is necessary, it is part of our growth. God has destinies unfurled in serving, whether at the family meal table, on the worship team, in the five-fold ministry, in the prayer closet or serving on the streets.

ALL service starts in Him, comes from Him, is through Him and unto Him. Jesus is our ultimate example.

We can however be overtaken by the need to serve and driven to serve for so many reasons, but as always, in all things, Jesus wants to set us free from those wrong motives or agendas.

Sitting and knowing the heart of Jesus, being in union with Him, and seeking His Kingdom first, as Mary did, is the example to guide us.

We may have thought that sitting and resting in Him, loving Him and being loved by Him, was secondary to pleasing Him with our activities, ministries and missions, but our life is about union, relationship, love, and connection with the heart of Jesus, *first*.

Our priority is Him.

Prioritise knowing Jesus over ALL other things.

As you do, He will release strategies and plans to move you forward, from His heart. You may be surprised that, while you rest, He will use someone in your life to do exactly what you could have done. Because that is their purpose. You would have gone on ahead to carry out your plans, overriding His, pushing others out of theirs, tiring yourself out and then a realignment would be necessary.

We could totally miss His heart and His purpose in all our activity.

We could miss the heart of the people in all our movement. Miss the hand to hold and the sharing of His mercy, had we remained at rest.

Our passion has driven us, sometimes to the detriment of others, because we so desire to see His Kingdom come forth. Moving like this, out of our own enthusiasms and passions, can cause us to become out of sync with His timing. Prioritising our own agenda, having wrong motives, could draw us into pride-based activity that has drifted too far from His heart.

And so, allow Him to draw you to His heart before you move out with a purpose, and be drawn to Him on a daily basis.

Allow Him to draw your heart into the secret place where He will minister great truth, revelation and healing to your spirit, soul and body. Accept His invitation to know the depths of His heart, as you reveal yours. Then, you will move when and where He moves, see what He sees and be all He has called you be. From a place of rest. From a place of contentment, and knowing fully, who you are.

Moving from His heart, allows you to know His timing, His agenda and His motive, and tunes you into being in the right place, doing the right thing, at the right time.

Our efforts in ministry are not wrong. The evangelism, the prayer meetings, the bibles studies, the worship team leading, the serving, the kitchen duty…none of it is wrong. It is all necessary.

But this is the hour where Jesus is re-ordering your priorities to make Himself number one in your life, so that He can open up the Kingdom and truly reveal HIS plans and purposes to you. And that which He has to reveal, your eye has not seen, nor has your ear heard.

Allow Him to position you every single day, as you lay down your life before Him.

Have you been running in circles getting busier and busier, with no results? This way of living doesn't line up with what you know you have been called to, in the depths of your being. You ask yourself the question, "Why is it all so hard???? Why don't I see results?"

You may be feeling an empty, nagging hunger, a deep thirst for more and Jesus wants to fill your hunger and your thirst now. But it will take a laying down of yourself. Total and complete surrender of all you thought you were, all that you think you are and all you think you are going to be.

This hunger for more of Him is satisfied in the Holy heart of a King who will accept nothing less than all of you. Isn't this what you long for? All of Him as He longs for all of you?

Seven

From Old to New

"This means that anyone who belongs to Christ has become a new person. The old life has gone, a new life has begun."

2 Corinthians 5:17 (NLT)

We walk in the newness of life in Christ, and are one with Him.

The devil has tried to keep our position as the beloved out of our reach, causing complicated theories and works based thinking as ways of attaining the fullness of Christ to rule and reign in our midst.

Now, those ways are being dismantled with the simple truth of The Gospel and the freedom we have when we believe, now being revealed to the laid down lovers of Christ.

Christ glorified, Christ in us, Christ, the hope of glory,

living and dwelling in us. His Kingdom comes on Earth as it is in Heaven, through our hands and hearts as we relinquish control to Him.

We are moving out of an old structure that has become stale and redundant to us, into a new realm of possibilities, where freedom reigns, The Blood displays the grace we walk in, where we move into the very heart of the King.

You might be feeling pressure in your heart and soul, as this move is taking place, but if you surrender your motives and agendas for the will of God, an acceleration will happen in the spirit, and all you have been thirsting and hungering for will be laid out on the banqueting table before you. Great peace will begin to permeate your soul, and the flow of your life will be astounding to you. I know this, because it happened to me.

If you continue to walk in old ways, trying to further the Kingdom by doing the same things you always have - thinking you know the way - this will lead into a journey that will take you through trials and testings you have faced before, but with a greater degree of heat. This also happened to me.

Obviously, I would choose the former over the latter any day and I am sure you would too.

Moving from the old way into the new is challenging, especially when the road has not been travelled before. We have become set in our ways, and can't see how the new fits with anything we understand, so we continue on in pride, stoic in holding our ground even as it crumbles beneath our feet.

Fear may become a companion in this time of change as we face the unknown. It is only in pressing into the heart of Jesus that we are strengthened to release and let go, for Him to fill our lives with new wine and fresh oil.

Fear is also a great driver into busy-ness. Being constantly on the move, going from here to there, tends to make us feel important. Some wear their constant activity as a badge of accomplishment, as they move about in their various roles, showing by their activities, how spiritual they are, and how mature they must be for God to be using them so much.

I can genuinely say this without judgment or condemnation, as I WAS such a person.

Perhaps there are some areas of your life Jesus would like you to surrender and let go, so that He can fill your life with new wine and fresh oil. This could be where you are overstepping your mark, into a position destined for someone else, OR He simply wants to draw you into the depths of His heart, and THEN lead you out from this new place into Greater Things. Whatever the reason, you may now be feeling a little pressure.

The purpose of pressure as we move from the old to the new is not to destroy, but to refine us in Holy fire, causing a purity to come forth. He sets His seal upon our entire being, the enemy will have no foothold in our life and destiny when we fully submit and yield to Him.

"….as you yield everything to this furious fire until it won't even seem to you like a sacrifice anymore."

Songs of Songs 8:7 (TPT)

His passion for you becomes so powerful that in drawing you to His heart, the pain of letting go, the fear of the future, of the unknown, all pale in comparison to yielding to the heat and feeling Him free you from the chains you have been pulling against on a daily basis.

Seek Him, seek His face, and exalt His name. In the pressure that surrounds this realm, as you keep your eyes fixed on Him, your heart melded with His heart, you will be able to withstand the fiery furnace of His love and come forth as gold.

Let the fire of His passion burn within you now, consuming you to the point where there is no distinction between where His world ends and your world starts. You belong to Him.

"Fasten me upon your heart as a seal of fire forevermore. This living, consuming flame will seal you as my prisoner of love. My passion is stronger than the chains of death and the grave, all-consuming as the very flashes of fire from the burning heart of God. Place this fierce, unrelenting fire over your entire being. Rivers of pain and persecution will never extinguish this flame. Endless floods will be unable to quench this raging fire that burns within you. Everything will be consumed. It will stop at nothing as you yield everything to this furious fire until it won't even seem to you like a sacrifice anymore."

Song of Songs 8:6-7 (TPT)

You have been crucified with Christ, yet you live.

Eight

Limitless in Yielding

"I have given you all authority to set the captives free, to open the blind eyes, to see deaf ears hearing, and to command the lame to walk. I have filled you with the knowledge of my will, and you are filled with the fullness of Me. It is my will that you lay hands on the sick and they recover. The power in the purity and simplicity of My words, and the work of the cross are being revealed into the hearts of the humble, into the hearts of those yielded to the movements of My heart. The power of My love is reaching into the very depths of my children and drawing out the greater works.

It is time for you to walk in the revelation of these simple words. I have set you free. Only believe."

God is the same yesterday, today and forever. This doesn't mean He is moving the same as He did yesterday, though often we get caught up in yesterday's moves.

I think of the account of the transfiguration on the mount, (Matthew 17) that involved Peter wanting to build a tabernacle for Jesus, Moses and Elijah. As he spoke his thoughts, God spoke from heaven, permeating the atmosphere with His presence.

I was once like Peter there, building an altar, getting carried away in the work, then missing the leading of God into the next phase. Distractions from what happened in the past can leave us wanting and in lack, disabled by our thoughts of how things should be, when Holy Spirit is going to reveal what He is going to do next!

The new wine, the fresh oil, the living water, all come from fresh, sweet, current revelation. Not from continuing to move in an old, stale way, waiting for the change to come, before *we* change.

In actual fact, we need to change before change comes. Which is exactly what is happening now.

We are being awakened.

Awakened and transfigured as new revelation is unfolding within the Body of Christ, and within our hearts. Our transformation comes as we lay down, in Shalom rest, surrender our mind, will and emotions to Jesus and allow Him to take control over our growth, our walk, our gifts, our ministries and our hearts.

Our transformation, as we enter into the Holy secret place, causes us to see with eyes of the Spirit, as we become aware of His indwelling Presence, and nothing can cause us to move from that place.

Nothing can separate us from His divine love that permeates our being, and we become undone by His movements in our heart. It is from here that we live and move and have our being.

We are shifting into the newness of life in Christ Jesus. Forgetting everything we have known so far. Forgetting our methods of prayer, our formulas for releasing the captives, and for building our own empires.

Now is the time for you to walk into the calling of your destiny, that which has been written in the book about your life, from a place of rest and peace in Jesus. From a place of contentment, knowing that we truly belong to Him, knowing that all is for Him, through Him, and to Him.

Jesus ministered this to me:

"I am calling you to a place of greater surrender, where I am free to move through you, unhindered by what you think, or who you feel you are not.

I now dispossess the enemy of all land and territory he has had in you, through the strongholds of your mind, and I relieve him of all he has taken illegally.

I evict him from the throne he has illegally set up in your heart and in your home.

The word of truth for your life is that you and your house will serve me. My Name is higher than any other name, and My name is exalted in your home, therefore I am drawing all men unto me, who enter into the realm and sphere of your influence.

Repent now, change your thinking, bring it into a higher realm to be in line with My thinking, that where the enemy has had legal right to enter into your heart and mind, that he may be expelled.

The Greater things I have called you to are released now through your simple belief that it is time, and that I AM able.

I have shifted my people from the realm of impossibility and limit, into the place of freedom and worship.

A realm of limitless possibilities. Begin to dream again as you absorb my heart and mind for you.

Be at peace. Be still and know that I AM GOD. I live in you. Be still in this. Selah.

Only in rest, learnt here, in this day, will you find the light and be the light in the days to come.

Absorb me. Absorb my nature. Be one with me as I AM one with my Father.

Internal peace radiates as a light to those in darkness.

In the midst of a chaotic world, peace exudes from my Shining Ones.

They are not shifted by circumstance, by wars, sick children, dying elderly.

My rested ones walk in fortitude and strength.

They have BECOME ONE with me, and walk in power.

They are the miracle workers, the dead raisers.

My rested ones exit the secret place in humility and strength.

They carry weight without pride.

They walk lightly with authority.

They know who they are

They know who I am.

We are ONE."

A Prayer:

"Lord, My God, the sweet honey of revelation and the nourishing truth of your constant Presence and shalom peace is what sustains us. There is no longer a need to hunger and to thirst. The invitation has been given, to come to the banqueting table, where your banner over us is love. We accept it Lord. Help us not be like those who refused the invitation to come to the wedding banquet.

We gaze in wonder at your face as you feed us from the abundance of your heart.

Fruits of repentance abound here. The wonderful, cherished gift of being able to turn from our carnal ways, to see with the eyes of Christ, undoes my heart, and we surrender to the grace streaming from your heart.

Thank you Father God."

Our actions and deeds, laid bare before Him, are now consumed at His table, by grace and forgiveness. There is no need to panic at the table of The Lord, where His Love covers a multitude of sins.

Honesty and a yielded heart laid bare, He has washed us clean to purity. The weight of trauma and pain lifts as we surrender to His gentle words of grace:

"Come unto me, all ye that labour and are heavy laden, and I will give you rest"

Matthew 11:28 (KJV)

As we move more deeply into intimacy, any issues, burdens, sins and idols we may have carried are consumed by His Holy fire that burns in every surrendered heart.

His loving grace reveals that which is within, so that we may turn and allow the sweetness of His Presence to cause us to think differently.

 In the revelation of truth brought about in the purification of our minds, we no longer believe the lies and deceits of the enemy. We no longer walk with our eyes clouded or dimmed by our experiences, no matter how painful or traumatic they were.

His all-consuming fire refines and purifies the very depths of our being.

And so… There is no need to strive or try to improve yourself. You are totally loved, and accepted in the beloved. Yield yourself to His loving hand and the anointing that breaks the yoke will flow from His heart into yours.

As we journey deeper together, I am about to bare my heart and my past for your scrutiny… But first let me prepare the way:

As the title of the book declares, we are moving from striving to sweet Presence. My story will reveal where I have walked, and also, what I have walked out of. Going deeper with me as you read, this may also stir some deep thinking on your part, helping you to be honest and true to yourself, as Holy Spirit gently speaks to you.

Within my testimony, you may see things about your own life which aren't so easy to acknowledge, but you are so important to Jesus that He wants you to go deep and be honest, to repent (change how you think), to have an open heart and attitude toward anything He reveals to you, as you too move into a new way of living.

My testimony is one of *overcoming* a pride-based, religious spirit, to walk in the freedom of encounters with Christ, encounters that have changed my life with Him, forever.

Jesus is calling us to take our eyes from ourselves, our abilities, charismatic character and strengths, and gaze upon Him.

The time has come for us to stop chasing after selfish ambitions, to stop pride from being in the drivers' seat. Ego is now put under the blood as we are drawn into a love walk with Jesus and we rest in Him, learning a new way of life, living and thinking, under the guidance of Holy Spirit.

Holy Spirit has impressed upon me that this isn't a "how-to" book, but that my testimony is to be shared to help make a way for others. Where we have forged a path, and leave it clear, others are then able to follow with less resistance coming against them.

The scripture in Revelations 12:11 says that we overcome by the blood of the Lamb and the word of our testimony and so, as you hear mine, open your heart, and yield to the touch of Holy Spirit. Perhaps He desires to pinpoint, convict (not condemn), and bring you to a new place of repentance and breakthrough too.

God has worked in me through a process of re-alignments and new thought patterns, to bring me to peace. He has stripped me of lies and deceits of the enemy, removing wrong thinking about who I am, and how I am to walk, and released me from bondages of the past which I had picked up throughout my years as a believer.

He is willing and able to do this for you too, as you surrender to our loving King, and allow Him access into the deepest recesses of who you are.

With your heart yielded and your eyes fixed on Him, He will begin to sovereignly move you, by His grace, into the fullness of all that the Gospel means.

Nine

My Testimony

Some start their lives knowing Jesus as Love. I didn't really recognise that until I was quite a long way down the track in my journey with God.

In my mind and at a surface level in my heart, I knew of His great support and love for me, I knew His kindness and grace and mercy.

Some start out with a basic understanding of Christianity being that of 'loving the Lord our God with all our heart mind and soul, and loving our neighbour as ourselves', as it says in Matthew 22:37, providing a dramatically changed perspective towards others. The carnal nature's way of competition, jealousy, envy and strife, fading into insignificance as the truth of who He is, and who we are in Him, causes genuine change.

Some of our walks didn't start in those ways. Mine began in a search for power.

I came out of a New Age lifestyle, which, despite all the talk of love and acceptance, was ruled and run by a spirit of competition and jealousy. There was an underlying competitive spirit that I carried through into my Christian walk and it took many years to displace in me.

Looking back, the effort to overcome these manifestations of the flesh led to overly focusing on what I felt was wrong with me, and not on what Jesus died for me to become.

I tried to change myself, instead of trusting in the Saviour to bring about the change I needed simply by standing in His Presence, in awe of His glory and light. This was such a powerful lesson and I would encourage you right now to begin gazing at your Beloved and the beautiful fruits of the Spirit, as you continue to read my testimony.

A side note - If I had been aware that walking in the fruit of the Spirit is actually manifesting Christ's nature, I wouldn't have just taught about it in Sunday School at the first church I was in, I would have pursued them wholeheartedly, to be like Jesus. This was not my number one priority then. It so totally is now.

Due to the prophetic gifting on my life, I was quickly respected as I moved in the gifts of the Spirit (which were genuine). My heart motive at that time however, was one of being seen and valued, not of Christ's voice being heard and acted upon.

I thank Jesus often, for being the remover of my shame, but at the time I relished being seen and valued, and walked in a position of authority, while being driven by a need for acceptance and love.

Once I realized I carried gifts that others looked up to, ego and pride stepped up nicely too. I fitted well wherever the same religious spirits were at work, which love to cause striving and where works-based ministry thrive. These things kept me out of true relationship with Christ.

Jesus was my life and love, but I was sitting squarely on the throne of my own heart at this point.

It felt good to have people honour me, want to talk to me because I was a leader, and look at me with respect.

I was serving in what I thought was humility, but it was false humility, driven by pride and a need to be seen. Undergirding all of this, I struggled with low self-esteem, which often presents as pride and arrogance because you carry a need to prove who you are.

I was not a threat to the Kingdom being revealed on earth, as I moved about with my own agenda, to exalt myself first and Jesus second. Truly, I was unaware of this, and despite it, God was kind and mercy abounded as He moved in and through my life in an awesome way. Yet there it was.

I really thought I loved The Lord with all my heart, mind and soul, and was totally unaware of the deception I was trapped in. This didn't mean Holy Spirit didn't use me. There were people around me who were hearing the voice of God through me, but the deep motives, and the way I was driven from my heart, He alone knew.

His lovingkindness surrounded me, and He upheld me in many ways. His love for me was not going to let me continue on the journey in this manner. His agenda is to heal ALL hearts, bringing us into greater purity and holiness. His love was constantly drawing me and I was constantly willing.

By the way, there were many lovely, nice things about me too, just so you know! I'm not on a 'down myself' little trip here.

I could see God working in my life, co-ordinating events, and placing people around me that I needed. He upheld me through some of the most difficult years of my life at that time, and I look back on it with such deep gratitude for the pastors, leaders, friends and brothers and sisters who have been on this journey with me.

Our lives are a tapestry of events and movements, each road leading to growth if we allow it to. Being gentle with ourselves when we see what needs to be changed is paramount to not allowing the devil a foothold. Condemnation, guilt and shame are weapons that can find a foothold, if you do not hand over your past to the Loving Saviour of your soul.

Be honest and transparent with Him, and with yourself, to gain true freedom.

The reason I share these things, baring my soul to friends and strangers alike, highlighting them, is because I know they will be touching a chord in many.

Holy Spirit resident within you, may now be convicting in His beauty and grace. Move with Him as is fit for your life right now, asking Him to reveal the wrong attitudes, distorted beliefs, and carnal ways of thinking. His love covers a multitude of sins as He journeys with us to bring us into complete fullness in Him. Hand them over to Him, in a returning of your heart to His.

Let Him re-align you back into His will now.

His mercy is new every morning. As you know, what you truly repent of NOW, is forgiven NOW.

Your mind is changed through repentance, now you can move forward. If there are modes of behaviour to change, well walk that out with Holy Spirit, being quick to capture every thought that exalts itself against the knowledge of your gained freedom.

Your thoughts are your choice, and you can now move into complete freedom, gaining authority over your mind, and pressing delete (thank you Liz Wright) on past ways of thinking - taking captive every thought that exalts itself against the knowledge of God - is paramount.

Jesus was in the midst, back in those days, changing me in many different ways, and holding me through the many storms in my life, but it took years for the fullness of Christ's love to begin to manifest in my life.

I moved in what I thought was truth and love. The person I was and how I operated in the Spirit flowed from the revelation I had at the time. And that's ok.

There is truth and then there is a greater depth of truth. Precept upon precept. I was walking in a measure of fullness, in my love for Christ, and I was understanding and releasing in measure, all that His love revealed to me at that time.

I was about to be shifted into a completely different place.

I snapped my Achilles Tendon while at a Graham Cooke conference in Auckland in 2014 and was unable to walk for 3 months. Unable to drive, or get to church (I live a distance out of town), a lift, had I wanted one, was difficult in that respect. But the truth was that I didn't want one…

Having operated in my own strength as a Christian for 10-12 years, running a physically tiring business, raising a family, which had many challenges in itself, as well as ministry, I was unexpectedly relieved to sit down and rest, with a good excuse to do so. I slept day and night for the first 6 weeks. I really did!!

It was during this time I came into an understanding that God actually wanted a relationship with me. I could sense His presence so deeply and profoundly, that I didn't want to leave the place where I had finally found myself:

In His presence and in rest.

This was the beginning of a phase of my journey with God that I will treasure forever.

It was a new beginning – one of many – in which I was being drawn by the Father's goodness, to experience Him, not just as a movement I belonged to, but as the living, life-giving, life-breathing force of creation. As the fullness of love, and the reason for my being, the one on whom I could rely, and lean on for strength.

He became a reality to me in my convalescence.

I have since come to understand that my growth and destiny are in the hands of God, and there is no need to strive and try to make it happen, when I allow Him to be in control.

This journey has had its twists and turns, growths and set-backs. But my future, my tomorrow and my today, are His. My growth is His responsibility as I lay at His feet, surrendered to His hand.

Your future, your tomorrow and your today are His. YOUR growth is HIS responsibility. Lay at His feet and surrender to His hand.

At this time, I was awakened to the very present nature of a very present Jesus. I had previous experiences leading me into this intimacy with Christ along my journey, and I will not negate the effects of His drawing me by the power of His Spirit. I did have a tendency though to give away what I had received, rather than a soaking in, getting to know, and going deeper with The Lord.

Then, convalescing, in an incapacitated state, ALL I could do was receive.

It was in this place I began to learn of the importance of rest and soaking.

Every single day became a joy, as I pressed into the heart of God from my bed, and He poured into me through the words of Graham Cooke.

I would pray, listening to the words of Holy Spirit and then read or listen to a message by this anointed man of God, and EVERY SINGLE WORD would be confirmed. It was such a time of confirmation of my ability to hear the voice of God.

Graham's conversations with Jesus inspired me, as I had been having conversations for years, but had not valued them for what they were. The treasures that were being imparted to me became real.

I was entering into a new and living way of being.

I was entering into relationship. This is what had been missing.

This had been the nagging void in my Christian life.

The striving and seeking for more, was being filled.

The works, deeds and self-seeking had not bought satisfaction.

 I was hungry and thirsty, and didn't know I was dying of starvation.

His grace had held me, His mercy had endured, because He knows the beginning from the end.

He saw where I was destined to be.

Ten

Idol of Ministry to True Rest

I discovered in that time of rest, that there is no need to go digging into your past to find the issues, making cavities where there are none.

Jesus will lead us into all truth, about Him and about ourselves.

He is kind and loving, though relentless. This is not to say that issues don't present. As we journey this life, He reveals the innermost thoughts and intentions of our hearts to us, without shaming or condemnation, and brings us to purity with the sword of the Word that separates between bone and marrow.

There is a need to be honest in our assessment of how we are travelling with Holy Spirit, and seek guidance and help from leaders and trusted friends if we need it.

Where situations are especially painful or traumatic, I have sought to pray with others to help me release and go through the process of re-aligning and allowing Jesus to restore my soul.

This is how we are destined to journey, as a body, being used of Jesus to encourage, edify, uplift, and restore one another with and to Him.

We need also, to be honest in our assessment of where we are as a body. Much has entered in that is not of God, and our Father is now in the process of stripping away what is false, prideful and ego-based. He is taking back what is His, and bringing us back to a place of humility and purity, and revealing His heart of love as His utmost desire for us.

This process is painful and will involve much disruption in the Body of Christ, as we know it.

Words seem hollow and meaningless when untouched by Holy Spirit, becoming painful in our depths, even embarrassing to hear and to bear, as no fruit comes forth.

We have puffed ourselves up with rhetoric and self-exaltation, with a hole growing on the inside, feeling more and more empty. But JESUS. But GRACE.

"Today I appoint you to stand up against nations and kingdoms. Some you must uproot and tear down, destroy and overthrow. Others you must build up and plant."

Jeremiah 1:10 (NLT)

We have built idols: ourselves, our churches, our ministries.

The superior way of this different era, is that we allow Jesus to be King, and we understand and walk into the truth that we are His Bride, highly valued and prized by Him, loved to our depths, and with no need to prove ourselves.

We abandon ourselves to the peace and righteousness of HIS way, without the striving and the trying that has plagued our journeys thus far. We need to get off the throne of our own hearts, and relinquish ourselves wholly to Him.

You may think you have already done this, but if you are not shining with His light, filled with deep peace and joy, walking about healing the sick, releasing the oppressed, I am really sorry to say, you may well be still sitting on your throne. Ouch.

When God begins a process of deconstruction in our lives, we can enter into a realm of fear, denial, excuses, blindness, deafness, out-right disobedience and rebellion. Yep - That's why the deconstructing has to happen!

The revival you have been waiting for is within the temple, of which you are.

So let the wrecking ball in.

Allow the dismantling of stale ministries to happen. Stop trying so hard to work up the power, without the power of the Spirit. Let it all go. And choose to trust Him.

It is difficult to hear the truth, no matter how it comes, and it's even possible you would like to stop reading this book right now. Please don't. It gets way better. Even skip to the final chapters if you need encouragement to allow Father God to have His way in your heart. (I did that!! I needed the encouragement to continue writing, because I understand this part of the book is heavy!!).

Anyway… you know you have been searching for something… that there is an unfilled void that you can't fill, and that you are still seeking for something you haven't attained yet.

Let God have His perfect way in you.

Continue to read, and see where He takes you in your Heart. Please don't be in a hurry. Sit with Him. Listen slowly. Listen from rest. Feel His drawing and pulling you into the depths of His heart, and allow the two-edged sword to begin to separate between bone and marrow. He is for you not against you.

In the light of these beautiful truths, Jesus gave me these words:

Lay Down

"So, lay down your plans, your hopes and your dreams,

And let me give you Mine.

Lay at the cross all that has seemed

To come from the divine.

You think you're not prideful, and set in your ways,

Yet you struggle and push in for more.

Let me lead you in my Holy way,

Come through my open door.

It's simple and easy, this may cause you to stumble,

How can what is so rich, be so free?

My breath that brings life, and freedom and flight

Was bought by my blood, do you see?

You try and you strive, having read your own scroll,

You know where you're headed - don't you?

Let me tell you now, that you've been so bold

But it's humility that will see you through.

You've been through the fire,

A character formed,

You walk with integrity, true.

But now is the time, the big test of your life,

Was it me, or was it you?

Did I bring you to this point, or was it your effort?

Did you walk alone, or were you carried?

Your effort was noble, you moved in the gifts,

But in my presence did you tarry?

Will you stand at my door and say I prophesied in your name?

And I'll have to turn you away?

It's not my desire to do that, or even, to cause you to cry in deep shame.

This is the reason you're dry and you're thirsty.

Your own wells you have dug very well.

Your efforts were cheered by others who saw, carnal nature exalting itself.

So when will you listen, and when will you learn,

To lay down your gifts and surrender?

Did you hear my voice and yet follow your own?

If your heart is still hard and not tender?

Come let us go to the mount of The Lord,

Turn, return, seek My face.

I draw you into My high tower,

The solitude of My Holy place."

If you have not already, now is the time to destroy the kingdom you have built in your inner world, in surrender and yieldedness, to the plans of God for your life.

In this place of surrender, Holy Fire is coming quickly to consume your sacrifice. So, it will not even seem a sacrifice anymore.

If you have destroyed the idols and the kingdoms, it is time now for you to marinade in the honey of fresh revelation and trust, with vision from HIS point of view.

The Podium…a Vision

I was in the midst of an immense crowd:

The way was parting before me as I walked toward the front, all the way to a mighty stage, up the stairs leading to the podium. As I reached a landing on the stairway, there appeared a wheelchair ramp to the right and Holy Spirit bid me to walk that way.

I was a little confused, even a bit offended, seeing that the stairs, not the ramp, went directly to the podium. I DID have a choice. I knew in my heart, that I could choose to walk directly up those stairs and would be standing in front of that cheering crowd.

One really cool thing about my relationship with Jesus is that He always impresses quite strongly which is HIS preferred way. So, in the vision I DID have the choice and I knew the wheelchair ramp was the way I needed to go. I walked up and it took me around the back of the podium.

This led me into a totally different space.

It was dark, quiet, peaceful.

It was secret. No one could see me.

This was the entrance into The Secret Place.

Holy…holy…holy

This was right at the beginning of another season in my walk with Yahweh. He was showing me where He was going to take me: Out of sight, and into the depths of Himself.

He removed me from any form of ministry, telling me to be silent, and not travel. Wow, that was a difficult time, as you could very well imagine. From being up front, being used in prophecy and bringing a word from God, to not stepping up at all.

I knew I could still use this gift, I was still prophetic, discerning and able to preach. But I also knew it was not what Father God was wanting of me at that time. This was a desert experience, where the need for the accolades of man began to die in me.

Ponder this for a moment - If all that you ever did, you did before an audience of one, would your heart toward God remain the same?

Let it be an encouragement to you, that at this stage of writing, having been through the process, all I want to do is be in front of the that one person audience. The striving and trying to please, or look good, or perform does actually die, when you are touched by The Creator of all things.

The secret place will first become a reality, and then a priority.

"Fasten me upon your heart as a seal of fire forevermore. This living, consuming flame will seal you as my prisoner of love. My passion is stronger than the chains of death and the grave, all-consuming as the very flashes of fire from the burning heart of God. Place this fierce, unrelenting fire over your entire being. Rivers of pain and persecution will never extinguish this flame. Endless floods will be unable to quench this raging fire that burns within you. Everything will be consumed. It will stop at nothing as you yield everything to this furious fire until it won't seem like a sacrifice anymore."

Song of Songs 8:6,7 (TPT)

Eleven

Lay Down the Old

I heard the Lord say:

"Hand me your keys…all you're able to do.

All your qualities, gifts and talents.

Partake at the table of presence where I'll feed you on cakes of raisins and life.

All that you need is right in My hand, all you require is my breath.

Breathe in the substance of life, deep into your lungs.

I have Heaven's air for you, unpolluted by greed, the seeking of fame, the rocks of jealousy and strife.

You don't need to perform, or be seen as one who is able.

I have the pure fountain, springing up from within, pouring forth to bring new life.

I have adored your heart for me, and how you have moved in the revelation you have had. You are my greatest delight, the reward of my suffering.

Now My love will remove from you all that did not flow from a pure heart, but out of an idol of self.

This may feel like utter destruction to you but is My purpose to fulfil the plans I have for your life.

I have so much more for you, and I am calling you to no longer live life based on who you appear to be before men, but on who you ACTUALLY are in me.

It is MY purpose for you to walk free of all ego-driven activity, all striving from lack of self-esteem and the pride which has driven you to become busier and busier, into the sweetness of My presence.

I long to pour into you from my pure well, replacing that which is beginning to ferment, bringing you into complete fullness.

Allow me access as you are emptied of your carnal nature and wrong thinking releases its grip.

You ARE the vessel of my choosing, and I HAVE a plan and destiny for you which goes far beyond everything you have ever thought or dreamed of.

You cannot make this happen yourself. I OPEN DOORS NO MAN CAN SHUT.

You are required to surrender your keys which have been hewn out of clay, for it is my desire to give you My Spirit, to ride the waves of the wind, free in ME.

This will feel like death, as you move from the self-reliance of your carnal nature, to full surrender. And so… It is."

"My old identity has been co-crucified with Messiah and no longer lives…And now the essence of this new life is no longer mine, for the Anointed One lives his life through me –we live in union as one!! My new life is empowered by the faith of the Son of God who loves me so much that he gave himself for me, dispenses His life into mine!"

Galatians 2:20 (TPT)

I heard the Lord say:

"I want you to receive the reality of these words into your innermost being. I live in you.

Allow the implications of this to permeate the depths of your soul.

Let me live through you.

I don't need you to reveal me to the world.

I will reveal myself through you.

I know you, and I know the desire of your heart has always been that this would be so.

Entwine your heart with mine, allow your thoughts to become one with mine.

I long to reveal myself to you, and trust you with my thoughts and plans.

Become one with me."

Twelve

Knowing our Purpose and Destiny

Much has been released in the Spirit over the past few years in regards to destiny. This touches our hearts on an emotional level, and our imaginations, as we dare to dream.

Our destiny ignites the flame of passion within as we seek to fulfil the purposes of God, which have been revealed through His word, His prophets and in our own heart.

This is Gods' idea.

It is His will that we know and walk out the plans and assignments He ordained for us from the beginning of the world. We were formed in our mother's womb, seeded by our father, from the heart of our Heavenly Father, with a destiny to fulfil.

When this begins to unfold before our eyes, through unfolding revelations, or encounters with God, as human beings, some of us tend to pick up the ball and run. We care not for process and engaging with others, but more on getting the job done. We know where we are going and how we are going to get there. Don't we?

PRESENCE

"The Secret place

My love pours out upon you,

As you sit in a baby's rest.

Liquid gold of flowing honey

Sweetness to the bereft.

To breathe me in, and breathe out pain

Healing oil flows.

The striving pain of trying hard,

With not much fruit to show.

The void being filled with precious grace,

As my presence lifts the fear

The questions in your heart held long

Can you carry all you hold dear?

You have moved to show my Kingdom,

Reveal me to the world,

But somehow lost the vision

When your scroll, to you unfurled.

You knew the plans and purpose,

You took them and you ran.

I wanted to go with you

But you left your lover's hand.

You thought you carried me with you,

When you ran ahead in pride

But now let's fix up that mistake,

As deep in me you hide.

Return my love, to where we began

Come back to the place of birth

Where you and I, we became as one

And you cherished every word.

Take your eyes now from the world,

Of works and fame and notions

Lift your eyes to the hills where I live

Begin again, with no motion.

Come and sit with me awhile,

Listen carefully to who I am

Let me reveal my heart in you

I have a brand-new plan

I will do it. I will run

And you can come with me.

I will show you how to move

And set the captives free

Through my eyes you will see what they need

Through your mouth the words will come

Not your own ideas and truths,

But revealing me, The Son

And only because you know me

Deeply acquainted with my heart

Because you spent time where I drew you

From loves bonds you don't depart.

So sweet the very presence now

You carry in Peace, no shame.

Under the shelter of my sweet love

Hidden in loves embrace."

I heard the Lord say:

"Come into the secret place where it is only you and I. This is where I AM your strength.

I am liquid poured out over you in the high tower of safety. You can be you here, in the intimacy of our relationship, forged in secret.

I know the very core of who you are, what makes you operate, and the motives and agendas behind every action.

There is nothing hidden from view. All you are is in plain sight to me, and as you acknowledge this, your heart will break in pieces.

Tears will flow, and healing will come. You have no need that man should teach you, but I will teach you, who I am, in the revealing of yourself and of your heart.

My healing anointing flows in the secret place of intimacy. Quiet. Be still and know that I am God.

Only breath, and peace. Tears and strength.

Your tears, and my strength.

Your heart's desire is truly to gaze, in wonder at Majesty.

Your heart's desire is to look and to see, who I am, and who I'll make you become.

My darling, my dear one, surrendered at last, with heart open wide you can see it is me who has drawn you, to my breast, to show you all you can be.

Come sit, let us talk. It's all that I want. To be with you, alone.

To abide in your heart, undivided in truth, to heal, and make you my home.

For you to know who I am, it's you whom I love. To see with eyes filled with love.

I want your attention, I want you to come, I want you, I want you, I want you…"

"Who has ever first given something to God that obligates God to owe him something in return? For out of Him, the sustainer of everything, came everything, and now everything finds fulfillment in Him. May all praise and honor be given to Him forever! Amen!"

Romans 11:35-36(TPT)

When we grasp with both hands, what we know in our hearts to be the purpose of God in our lives, the first stepping stone involves handing it back to Him. Ouch.

Our journey from right here, right now involves walking with Jesus. His greatest desire for our lives is not that we do great and mighty things for Him. It is that we walk with Him to get there.

His heart is for relationship with Him, and to unveil and reveal His nature through us to others. To steward the gift well, the destiny with integrity, means standing inside of Him, moving when He says, and being still when He is still.

Thirteen

Some Body Work

As we transition from works to rest, there are some things we can do to help ourselves:

- Be easy, and kind with yourself
- Do not allow the devil of condemnation to wrestle with your soul
- Spend time in nature, absorbing creation at its finest
- Colours will become brighter as you step into the heart of Jesus, and enjoy with him
- Enjoy your family and re-build relationships that have suffered over the years
- Breathe
- Breathe deeply.

Learn to re-set, day by day, turning the eyes of your heart to Jesus within you, and focusing on Him.

Jesus is the centre of all things and He wants to be the centre of your attention, your eyes turning and re-turning to His Presence within you, throughout your day.

Allow Holy Spirit to blow away the debris of broken dreams, fatigue and confusion that hangs around times of transition.

You are now being realigned so your thinking is the thinking of Christ.

Trust Him with all your heart mind and soul, and lean not on your own understanding now.

"Now God has offered to us the same promise of entering into his realm of resting in confident faith. So we must be extremely careful to ensure that we all embrace the fullness of that promise and not fail to experience it. For we have heard the good news of deliverance just as they did, yet they didn't join their faith with the Word. Instead, what they heard didn't affect them deeply, for they doubted. For those of us who believe, faith activates the promise and we experience the realm of confident rest!"

Hebrews 4:1-3 (TPT)

Unbelief is a busy place to live, a place of striving and trying to prove ourselves, requires much thought and attention.

Living in Faith is patient, enduring and calm. Resting is, indeed, a faith-filled position of our hearts.

We can be busy, but living from a place of rest. We can have ministries, businesses, families and responsibilities, yet still be connected at a deep level with Jesus. The awareness of His constant presence brings this rest to the forefront of our minds, rather than allowing the cares of this world to steal away what has been deposited deep within.

Fix your cares on Him, trust Him to lead you through this time of transition, and into the birth of your destiny.

He who has begun a good work in you will bring it to completion.

Rest into this.

Relaxing and breathing is important, because you are shifting from being driven. Your body needs to adjust as well as your soul.

I did some light research (not my strong point), into adrenal glands, re-setting the Vagus nerve, and breathing techniques to help me begin to exist at a slower pace. The temptation to find the next thing to do, work on, fix, re-build, or remove, was so great, Father God took me away from home at times to make me sit down.

I am an ideas person, always looking for things to do, making plans and constantly on high alert. This is something I am still learning to journey with. It's part of who I am. The essential place of rest is where I get to find out what are Gods' ideas, and what are mine.

Having the fruit of patience is paramount.

A lot of people who have strived and performed and 'moved' for God, like me, out of their own strength, are visionary and planters of works. God's ideas. Not just their own.

Coming from His presence, having been filled in the secret place is the only way, when your mind is bombarded with strategies and plans, resting is the God-ordained way for ministry.

"Be Still, and know that I AM GOD;"

Psalm 46:10 (NKJV)

Fourteen

The Bridge

"Then, by constantly using your faith, the life of Christ will be released deep inside you, and the resting place of his love will become the very source and root of your life."

Ephesians 3:17 (TPT)

There are days when it isn't easy to yield.

There are ways of behaving that need to change, but it isn't my job to look for those ways. It is my job to partner with Holy Spirit when He reveals behaviours, limiting beliefs and wrong thinking, taking measures to then come into alignment.

The point here is, we don't need to search for what is wrong with ourselves. We look at Him and let Him flood us with His love, then our behaviour changes, and choices that we make change, as we love Him and He loves us.

Coming into a knowing that I am not a disappointment to Him, that I am not letting Him down has changed my life. It has caused His love to become the source of my life. Not the activities, but Him.

So now we get to sit with Jesus, in absolute peace, knowing we are loved and accepted. We get to sit in perfect peace, which feels like lovely sweet honey, entwined in His love.

It is from here that Jesus will lead us into a vision or impressions of how either He sees us, or how we see ourselves.

For the most part, when this journey of surrender begins, there is a vast canyon of differences in the two opinions concerning ourselves. The Master changes us as we see these visions, or He impresses on our heart His own desire, over ours. He destroys the yoke of bondage with His anointing and sweet presence.

Once a wrong belief system or limited thinking is revealed, and the behaviour manifests in our lives through circumstances and triggers, we are presented with the opportunity to yield. We get to hand it over to Jesus, and take what He has to offer in return.

At times this can take a discipline lasting days or weeks, with our minds being renewed by the washing of The Word. We take every thought captive that is trying to exalt itself against the knowledge of God.

We are told in Philippians to fix our minds on things

above, not on things of this world. As we now walk as new creations in Him, we get to think like He does. Our soul (mind, will and emotions) gets to be parented by our spirit man, as the order of government is changed in our lives.

We are no longer governed by our carnal nature but by the Spirit, as we walk through all circumstances, because His words says:

"We have the mind of Christ." 1 Corinthians 2:16 (NIV).

Now we can acknowledge, pray, and move on in peace. The relief this brings is beyond description and will catapult us to a place of such freedom, and joy, we will never be the same.

Poverty is replaced by gratitude, criticism by love, offence by grace, my somewhat tainted eyesight by Jesus' vision.

Impatience is replaced by patience, that also comes with joy!

This became very evident to me one morning, when I had a hair appointment. I live 30km from town, and had left a little early to do some shopping. On parking I realised I had left my wallet at home. Perhaps it was the relief of not having to do the shopping, or the fact I was saving some money, but the trip home to get money was done with great joy, in worship, rather than berating myself for the mistake. The presence of peace in the car as I returned to town, filled me with such gratefulness that the 60 km roundtrip was not even on my mind. Only Jesus!!

As the glorious fruits of the Spirit manifest, and Revelation like honey flows forth from the throne of grace, my eyes are opened to, not only Christ in me, but Christ in you also. The entwining of my heart with His becomes such a reality that there is no need to prove through works, movements or actions, who I am in Him.

"For who has ever intimately known the mind of the Lord Yahweh well enough to become his counsellor? CHRIST HAS, AND WE POSSESS CHRIST'S PERCEPTIONS!!!"

1 Corinthians 2:16 (TPT)

Fifteen

Relationships

When you lay everything down, and continue to love - even through tears of hope deferred and lost and broken dreams - the desire to move out of that intimate place where it is all HIM, and only HIM, becomes a foreign concept to you.

If your heart's desire is to be close to His heart, at first it will seem that leaving His presence and walking again in the natural world is a wrench.

You long to be alone with Him again. Communicating with others, even those closest to you, becomes an intrusion of sorts. This only lasts for a while, as you adjust to your inner world, and Jesus begins to permeate into your natural realm of existence.

The intimate chamber remains intimate, and the longing to be there remains, but as you become infused with the fragrance of His love, peace journeys with you. You are set apart and holy unto Jesus. He will continually draw you with His jealous zeal for you.

There is a certain vulnerability, and lack of being able to communicate with others that comes with stepping out of the secret place, in the beginning.

There is so much sweet honey treasure within, and to find someone who is not going to trample on the beauty of holiness from whence your internal life is now flowing, puts you into an isolation which can be unfamiliar for some.

The need for words and general conversation becomes a chore, and to be in relationship apart from those closest to you may seem difficult. You are not the person you were before.

In this season, there is such rapid growth, shifting, and realigning, that you seem to be changing every single day.

You are being made new, forged in the beauty of holiness, transforming in His presence, and becoming a new creation in Christ.

Don't pressure yourself to move out from this beautiful cocoon of grace.

All you have ever desired, that which was seeded into you as your destiny, before you were born, is growing as a beautiful child is formed in his/her mothers' womb.

Don't abort the process through bowing to the ungodly expectations of man. You may find, over this time, some relationships will not last the distance. It could well be a season of renewal in this area, as you distance yourself from that which pulls or is a strain to continue in. Don't be hard on yourself over this. Allow Holy Spirit to be your guide, and gently let go of those that you need to.

It is a reality that some find it difficult being in a church setting. The traditional 4 walls. I actually believe there are some people who aren't in churches right now, because what they carry is being protected in the secret place of The Most High. It is being polished and honed to perfection as they deeply seek His heart without distraction, or a need to prove themselves. Some have been deeply hurt, and trauma holds them in. There is a tendancy to look upon these people from within the walls of the church as rebellious.

If we honor ALL members of The Body of Christ, without judging how they partake of relationship with Him, unity will flow and healing, from Love.

I have been on both sides of this. Neither place is wrong and neither place is right.

It took me a long time to find people marching to the beat of the same drum. I know there are many people who are walking with Jesus who feel they do not fit anywhere.

I would like to just say here, when the isolated ones begin to walk out in the community with the love they have been infused with, the world will change, and many will flock to the 4 walls, which will essentially begin to come down. House to house, His Spirit will flow, churches will not contain what He is doing, and many homes will open to catch the overflow of abundance He is pouring out.

I do all that I do for Him, and I know that is your heart also. That includes doing some things I don't actually want to do. Our feelings, and what has happened to us in the past have nothing to do with where *He* wants to go to further His Kingdom, in us and through us.

If you are being called from the secret place, back into community with other believers, do it with complete trust that Jesus knows what He is doing. He strengthens you for all things, not only for your good, but for the good of those around you, who need the aspect of God's heart that has been implanted within you.

What we carry is most likely the very thing that is needed in that place, and also the very thing we need, ourselves, to move forward.

Pride needs to lay down and as you choose to go where He says go, even if your mind, will and emotions are screaming against it, let Him direct you. He may just surprise you.

He knows His plans for your future. Decide to trust Him.

When all you have has been given over and you have found the heart of Jesus, it is only His will that comes forth.

Fruits begin to grow. All you have longed for passes away as you marvel at the character of Christ forming within you.

Patience takes her place in you, and joy bubbles from the inside. What irritated once, now doesn't warrant a thought. Situations and circumstances that seemed mountainous are now levelled, in the existence of holiness.

Spending time in the secret place yields benefits of comfort to your soul, that you never would have dreamed possible in all your striving ways.

The need to control every situation and manner of events is passed over to His hands, and He takes the wheel with competence. The things you thought you had to drive and steer are now fully His, and He knows the direction to go and how to arrive at the desired end.

If we look at this in terms of relationships, the need to coach, lead with wisdom and teach, now comes from a place of acceptance and love of self and others.

We begin to see with the eyes of Jesus and move with grace and gentleness. His nature shines forth as loving kindness, and words of encouragement flow, not as a teaching lesson, but from the fountain of acceptance. Acceptance of the fact that it is not our job to change anyone or anything. The pressure is taken away to 'help' those around us to maturity. That is the job of our Creator.

Glorious Holy Spirit ushers forth from within, breathing out life, igniting passion, switching on ideas and plans from the thoughts and intents of God heart, with the sweet honey of revelation from His throne.

His hand has bought us to life, His breath gives us life, and His guidance is available to all.

His words flowing through us have no attachment to the need for a person to listen and heed as a validation of who we are.

The way of life that Holy Spirit lays out in gentleness through our mouths, gives a freedom of choice. Filled with His light, those seeds sown in gentleness, humility and love, are now His, to water and grow.

"Pleasant words are a honeycomb sweet to the soul and healing to the bones."

Proverbs 16:24 (BSB)

We continue to sow seed, and water and harvest as He leads us, but the outcome is not our responsibility. The actions of others, are not ours to change. Whether the seeds grow, or fall by the wayside, this responsibility lies with those receiving the seed.

Resting back into the consciousness of who Jesus is in us, and who we are in Him: peace-filled, authority-packed carriers of His nature, this allows us to rule and reign without the need to control and dictate.

There is much Jesus wants to show us about ourselves that can only be revealed when we are in a body of believers. He wants to reveal you, and let you shine, and He wants to polish you. Which is what you want isn't it? I'm sure it is.

Walls are being broken down in relationships as we begin to understand our journeys are far more intertwined than we ever thought. We truly are part of the Body of Christ.

We are one IN Him, and we are one WITH Him. The entwining of our hearts with Jesus, causes us to become one as a body of believers. I am in Christ, you are in Christ, we are joined in Christ.

Honouring one another for who we are in Him, and seeing each other through His eyes, enables His Spirit to flow freely. Personally, I know that where there is honour, the gifts of the Spirit are turned on like a tap. When we honour, we draw out Christ within our brothers and sisters.

A great number of the difficulties that we face are within the area of communication, and how we love each other.

We have no right or need for unforgiveness or offence. Actually, we don't have the luxury for either, and I am sure you already know this.

Repent, as you know how, turning your heart back to God, and choosing to walk in love. Let Jesus heal your heart with His great love, and ask Him for a friend.

As He goes before us, and is our rear guard, He stands between us and our yesterdays. His healing balm is our portion and our cup today, as we put our blinkers on and gaze only at Him, as our Saviour, we journey together, individually, as one in Him.

Looking at Jesus, connecting with Him, brings us into union with the Godhead. This leads us into deeper relationships with one another, as His life flows forth into ours, restoring broken hearts, and healing our souls. This is so we can be known by our love for one another, and the world will see Him through us.

I am part of an amazing spiritual family called the International Mentoring Community (IMC), founded and run by Liz Wright. It is through her testimonies, experiences with Jesus and impartations from those experiences, that her guidance has bought me to a place I am now able to walk being set free from religion, striving, ego-based activities, man-pleasing, and the low self-esteem and self confidence that drove those behaviours.

I couldn't have walked this road alone, (though God knows, I tried), and Jesus gave me this amazing group of believers, who are nothing other than an encouraging, uplifting, unified, gracious, majestic, power filled, arm of the Bride of Christ.

In this group I get to see what the Bride of Christ looks like and am blessed and empowered every day in a walk of love and unity.

Through the IMC I have connected with Julie Brown, who has been so instrumental in the writing of this book. If you have a book in you, get in touch with her. After a profound encounter with the Proverbs 31 wife, the revelation that she is a type of the Bride was released and Julie founded The Proverbs 31 Movement, to bring the Bride into all the fullness of her potential. The Bride is to release the power of the creativity of Jesus as she helps others establish ministries, businesses and first time authors to release their books!

Jesus has used Julie's ministry and the friendship of others from around the world to propel me into the next phase of my journey with Christ. For these relationships I am eternally grateful.

It is only through these experiences that I can say, with great conviction, that relationships in the body are a magnificent, blessed fruit of relationship with Christ. We get to learn how to see one another through His eyes, and hear with His ears in the environment of the Ecclesia.

Divisionary walls are being dismantled. The Love of Christ which covers a multitude of sins, and floods our hearts, is causing God to manifest His nature on Earth, as it is in Heaven.

We are being changed from one degree of glory to the next, as we surrender with yielded hearts and minds to His love. No longer dictated to by this denomination or that, but moving in intimacy with Holy Spirit, and in oneness with one another.

There is a blending together of beauty as Anglicans meet with Baptists, Catholics with Pentecostals, Evangelicals with Charismatics.

There is a new sound coming forth as unity manifests within the body, as we, ourselves, unify with the heart of our Bridegroom King.

Our differences are giving way and allowing Jesus to change and transform us, His way.

I pray you get to know who your tribe is, if you have been walking alone, that you will know from which table you wish to partake of, as the substance of Christ is released through various nutritious ministries, online, worldwide, and in your local church.

I heard someone preaching a few months back about the power of unified prayer. He gave an illustration of a gateway, that one person in worshipful prayer will open one gate into the Kingdom of God, that His will be done on Earth as it is in Heaven.

A church, or group of unified Saints will open floodgates from the Kingdom of God, for His will to flood the Earth.

Sixteen

He Moves Through You

He is Always the Same

"As I change you, I am Lord in you.

My power in you is not diluted as I reveal your condition.

I AM just as powerful and ready to work through you

when I am refining you, as I am when you feel worthy.

Walk in the spirit, and be led by My Spirit – not by your feelings.

When you dwell in how you feel, your soul only hinders the outworking of my power.

Because you allow it to.

I AM ALWAYS THE SAME. READY TO HEAL AND SO WILLING TO."

I was born again in a Revival tent in Griffith, New South Wales, Australia.

I had been fairly deeply involved in a New Age/Wiccan lifestyle at the time. I was seeking truth, and it came in the form of Jesus Christ manifesting Himself in this tent for me.

I had been seeing a chiropractor for 8 years or more, on a fortnightly basis, for a problem I had in my back since I was born.

On the night I was born again, Holy Spirit washed through me, revealing Himself as the power over all things, my Healer, and my Lord. An Aboriginal Pastor, who lived a few hours north of Griffith, stepped out in front of the congregation with a strong word of knowledge for me.

At the time I was a sceptical unbeliever, only there because I felt if I had missed what was going on in the tent over the road from where I was living, I would miss my birthday.

This was the very thought I had during the day, watching the meeting being set up. I had arrived there with a crystal tightly held in my hand, to protect me from deceit.

This Pastor came out the front, with a word for healing teeth. My teeth had been inexplicably wiggly for a week. I didn't respond.

He gave the invitation to come forth again.

Again, I didn't respond.

The final time he said, "You need to come out now and receive your healing." He said it with such intensity and strength of purpose, I thought he was going to come and get me.

I went forward to surrender my life to my Saviour, with the Holy Hand of Christ pressing on my back as I walked forward. This was an experience I treasure in the depths of my heart.

When I got to the front of the meeting, the pastor put his hand out, pointing at me. "Is that you?" He asked with such intensity, I was a little afraid. "Is that you??" He repeated himself.

At that moment, I fell to the floor under such a powerful anointing from God, with a white light washing through me. I'm not sure how long I was on the ground for, but it was light when I went down and dark when I got up. Perhaps an hour. I had never seen such a thing in my life, but as I rose up, my teeth were healed, and I never paid another visit to the chiropractor again.

Looking back at the wonderful way I was born again, seeing afresh the truth that He moves through us even while we are being refined, Jesus and I had the following conversation:

I asked Him, "So, the man ministering in the revival tent, who healed my back, he would have been dealing with issues and yet you used him?"

Jesus' reply was this:

"The man *who healed your back? That Man was* **Me**. *A minister believed in MY POWER to heal and* **I** *moved through him, despite his soul's pain and anguishes. BECAUSE HE KNEW I COULD DO IT THROUGH HIM, the man ministered that night, using MY knowledge and MY faith to move your mountain. He trusted MY abilities. Do you?"*

"I have been crucified with Christ; and it is no longer I who live, but Christ lives in me; and the life which I now live in the flesh I live by faith in the Son of God, who loved me and gave Himself up for me."

Galatians 2:20 (NASB)

Moving forward now, powered by the Spirit of God, revelation knowledge and understanding floods my soul to believe in fullness in the one who dwells within me, and how I relate to that.

I relinquish all thoughts of my inabilities (and still do this now), as I surrender to Him as the power source.

It is Christ in me who works the miracles, sets the captives free, and pushes out the demons. I don't need to be perfect to pray for the release of a drug addict from addiction, or for anxiety to leave a depressed friend. I just need to believe in the power of Christ to do it through me. I choose to live by faith in HIS ability, not my own. Doesn't that relieve the performance pressure??!!

"It is no longer I who live, but Christ who lives in me..."

Galatians 2:20 (AMP)

Seventeen

Moving with Christ's Heart

"Then may your awakening breath blow upon my life until I am fully yours. Breathe upon me with your Spirit wind. Stir up the sweet spice of your life within me. Spare nothing as you make me your fruitful garden."

Song of Songs 4:16 (TPT)

There is a desire in us that goes deeper than ourselves. The substance of a call to something greater. As we are drawn deeper into Him, we are filled with His fullness. We are satisfied with the water from the well. And we yearn for more. More of this life-giving water, addicted to the Presence and Heart of The King, peace and joy being our portion.

This is a true way of life now, as we enter into the realm of possibilities, unhindered by shackles of performance and striving, moving from a place of rest, and not concerned with the opinions of man.

We are being filled with His fullness, and the difficult processes now pass away for glorious relationship-based living, where we are consumed by Him, enfolded in and enraptured by His love.

As we are filled with fullness, and our eyes are illuminated to the truth of the GOOD NEWS GOSPEL, we keep our eyes fixed on the good thing, the pure thing, the lovely thing before us. Christ in us, the hope of Glory.

We decide to believe for the best, seek the best and have faith for the promises. There may still be pain, and there will still be valleys, but our eyes are now fixed on Him who is more than able, as the way we traverse the difficulties is so different from the past.

His love enfolds us, as doubt and unbelief give way to complete trust, in the presence of His Love.

We no longer operate from paradigms of unbelief or for the glory of man. We no longer operate from realms of fear and past hurts. ALL of this has been removed by the power of the Cross, and we are entering into a time of governmental rule and reign, which requires us to know fully who we are.

Insecurity is being shifted out for confidence.

As people you have known for years begin to change around you, you celebrate Christ in them rising up.

Pray for them, also, to be filled with the fullness of God, and blessed with every spiritual blessing in heavenly places. This will also become your portion and your cup, as you reap what you sow.

All vestiges of jealousy and insecurity are pushed out of your life, by your declaring the light and life of Christ into those around you. Celebrate and praise God for His victory in lives around you, and gather up any pain that lingers in your carnal nature - placing it in His arms - while loving yourself in the process. (Thank you Liz Wright!!)

The unbelief is pushed out as we gaze at Christ. His light, love and life fill us, and we move into authenticity.

I was sitting next to a lake in the stillness of the evening. Watching the baby ducks, and abundant wildlife, I asked Jesus what He liked best. "Reflections," was His answer. I suddenly became aware of the beauty of the gum trees and blue sky mirrored in the water.

We become Christ-like in our nature, as we gaze into His beauty, and we are transformed by the washing of The Word.

We become what we focus on.

"I gaze face-to-face, that I may know me, even as I have always been known!"

1 Corinthians 13:12 (The Mirror)

This season is transforming us, as the absolute truth of these words begin to permeate into our innermost being.

As we gaze at the Majesty of Jesus, we become majesty.

As we gaze at, we become wise.

As we gaze into the eyes of Forgiveness, we become forgiving.

We are gazing at Love and reflecting Love, we are gazing at Freedom, and bringing freedom into our realm of influence.

We begin to walk with majestic confidence, as His Bride being revealed on Earth.

As our existence becomes more deeply and intrinsically linked with Jesus, through the surrender of our own ways, purposes and agendas, the Kingdom of God manifests more fully on this earth, through us, and in what we carry.

This is not a prideful way to think, it is a fact of glorious truth, that Christ in me the hope of Glory can produce the results He intended, if I believe in Him and I believe in who He says I am.

A reflection of His Love. His Bride.

Living as a temple of Holy Spirit, we walk in the power of our creator God, from an internal place of relationship, knowing who He is, and knowing and accepting who we are in Him. It's personal!!!

I was in a prayer of silence, deeply involved in loving Jesus one day recently, when He took me into a vision:

I was next to a pool. It was golden and glistening, and He bade me to walk into it with Him. I lay down in the pool of golden liquid, realising as I did, that it was honey. (I know my Mum will be laughing at this, as she knows how paranoid I have been all my life about sticky things…quite amusing that Holy Spirit chose this medium to speak so deeply in my life).

I lay soaking in this hydrating, nourishing substance, resting in Jesus arms.

He said He was going to put my head under. Momentarily this panicked me, due to the 'sticky aversion,' but it's Jesus, and how can I resist?!

As my head went under the liquid honey, I could feel my soul flooding with sweetness. I felt like I was breathing and drinking at the same time, and healing entered my body, my mind and my spirit. I was utterly refreshed in this experience, and even now, writing this, I can feel that refreshing of my spirit man once again.

You can receive this same refreshing for yourself, as you now breathe in the spirit of prophecy in this testimony…take a moment…

This is the honey of His presence. This is the sweetness of soaking in Him, and surrendering to His love.

This is the glory of it being personal.

We turn our eyes upon Jesus, turning our hearts to Him, in simple recognition that He is present. In faith we believe it, and the substance of this truth begins to manifest. First in peace. Acknowledge the peace. Be aware and rest for moment at a time in it.

As you begin to honour Holy Spirit manifesting, your awareness will heighten to His presence. You become what you look at, remember?

We are the Bride of Christ. The revelation of union and oneness, intimacy and relationship, is what has been on the heart of Yahweh for all of time.

It is in the depths of this union that He pours out the sustenance of His love. It is in the depths of this union that He reveals the secrets of His heart to His Bride. He reveals Himself to those who intimately connect with Him.

"I will give you the treasures of darkness, and the hidden riches of secret places, that you may know that I, the Lord, who call you by your name, am the God of Israel."

Isaiah 45:3 (NKJV)

His invitation has been extended to enter into the depths of His heart, and it is only there that you will find what you are looking for.

The surrender and laying down is only the beginning. Just as the Bride on her wedding day relocates to live with her husband, so we too are being called into a relocation:

Jesus is saying:

"Come and live in My Kingdom. This is where you will see your value as you gaze at me and I infiltrate your heart and soul with Love. The understanding of who you are will permeate your innermost being.

I will watch with the deepest affection, pride and joy, as you come into the glory of knowing yourself. Confidence will ooze from you, as you are spun around my heavenly dance floor. Joy will flow, as you swing on the galaxy swing seat. Peace will flood forth as you bathe in the pool of honey revelation.

As you begin to see as a reality the places I take you in the spirit realm, the manner in which you walk in this earthly realm will change. There is a joining together, as we meld as one, walking in union, that brings my presence, my ways, my truths, to Earth, as it is in Heaven.

Enjoy me, and from this place of enjoyment, I will move you forward with greater responsibility to rule and reign in Heavenly places.

Rest in me, and from this place you will have the authority to speak to mountains and they will be moved.

As you begin to trust me, and allow me to direct your life, bit by bit, piece by piece, you will gain confidence in me, as I have confidence in you.

This is being satisfied with marrow and fatness."

Jesus wants to fill you with the sweet revelation of His heart, fully given over to you, for you to explore and find yourself within its depths. This yielded surrender and intimate connection is where you get to know who you *truly* are.

This intimacy is where your future is seeded into the depths of your very being.

Immoveable from joy, unshakeable from peace, rooted in patience and endurance, showing lovingkindness and generosity. Walking in the light as He is in the light, you are shining His Love and nature to the world.

Being one with Christ in the secret place, and being fully aware of that oneness and completion in Him when you are living in the day-to-day activities, this is how we live and move and have our being in Him. Always choosing to be aware of Him.

As we walk through life, and life hits us with adversity, sickness and trials, we choose to be aware of Him. We engage with His presence within. This takes practice, and for most is a complete change of lifestyle.

Every day we get the opportunity to bring Christ into our circumstances, and engage with His ways of thinking. We get to be the window that people look through, where they catch a glimpse of a loving God they may never have even heard of before.

Yield, trust and listen. Bind yourself to The Lord, entwine your mind with His.

Great things are happening, as you allow yourself to be positioned by The King, realigned and moulded in the depths of His heart. Do not fear.

God is taking us into greater realms of authority and Government, so it is essential we are joined to Him and our eyes remain on Him.

When we fix our eyes on His sovereignty, the chaos and destruction of worldly circumstances are not so hopeless.

Our prayers and intercessions become worship filled and we KNOW He is in control.

Desperation and hopelessness, anxiety and fear, become foreign to us as we do not look to the left or to the right. Our influence, in the natural and the supernatural becomes greater, because it is untainted by fear of the future.

This is the walk of a Bride who trusts her husband.

This is what we turn back to when circumstances and trials hit us. This world and its troubles are not easy to walk in, but we have been born into the Kingdom for a time such as this.

For myself, I choose life, and to seek and pursue life. There is so much for us to go after in the spirit realm right now, coming from the heart of Jesus, why would we look to anything else?

If you do not know your first love with a passion and are not discerning from that place of relationship, the authority you carry in Him will be diminished.

Turning your heart back into Christ will ensure that you are not agreeing with fallacies set up to side track you, and your place of Bridal Governance remains steady in Him.

Eighteen

A Different Language

This is a word, with an accompanying scripture, that Jesus gave me as I sat next to Him on a garden seat, in the spirit realm:

"This is where miracles are born. Above the storms. Use the power of my Word. Speak it to me. Not pleading with me, or shouting it to me. Communicate my Word to me. We will talk about Shalom, we will talk about joy, we will talk about walking in the light together, we will talk about governance, and crowns, gateways and scrolls.

There is no need for you to war in a manner you have in the past. I have said you are seated in Heavenly places in me. Move from Heavenly places. Speak from there. It is from Heavenly places I will teach you how to govern in a way you have never experienced before.

I uphold you with the word of my truth, and sustain you in my strong tower. Don't strive and try to move like others. In quietness and confidence, you have your strength. Learn my ways from my heart, before all else.

Come for the honey of revelation knowledge of who you are and who I am, before you begin to move again.

I am showing you great and mighty things you have not seen before, as I trust you with my heart. I will allow you into the treasuries of insight and wisdom, and when you move out from my heart, carrying My presence, you will speak with words of revelation and knowledge.

This is the fruit of abiding in the vine. Many will come and partake of the fruits and spices, you have tended in our garden of love."

"Come, all my friends – feast upon my bride, all you revelers of my palace. Feast on her, my lovers! Drink and drink, and drink again…"

Song of Songs 5:1 (TPT)

"Your eyes are clear now, and you can see with great clarity. The hunger and thirst you have yielded to, implanted by Holy Spirit, drawn by The Father, and made possible through Me, have bought you here to this special place.

This is the new beginning, where you can come as my beloved and get to know me in a way you haven't known me before. Intimate in knowledge, as I reveal myself to my lovers."

And so, bringing nothing of the past, having laid it at the cross, much may seem unfamiliar to us now.

The old tool belt of go-to prayers won't sound so powerful, and training in a new language is necessary. The Kingdom has its own language, as it is a different realm of existence. It isn't all-knowing, competitive or hurried. This language allows you to contribute, talk quietly, laugh joyfully and sit peacefully as acceptance and awareness of our inner value begins to permeate our beings. Our eyes are opened, without pride, to see who we are and also see those who journey with us in the light of Christ.

Every person is undergirded in love and acceptance. Every heart is tended, cared for and nurtured. We are fully loved and respected here, just for being a lover of The King. There is a oneness and unity in this place, where words are often unnecessary, communication is pure, and Christ is central, in and through each one of us.

As each one begins to walk in the fullness of Christ, experiencing His Presence within, our identity settling in our hearts, we become a table for others to eat from.

We are to enjoy the delicacies of Christ's heart, revealed through every member of His body, bringing revelation, unity and peace.

Nineteen

Return and Remember

Now we no longer strive to be seen by man, because we know we are seen by Jesus. He is our breath and our life. All that matters in this world is this revelation.

"My Beloved is mine, and I am his;…"

Song of Songs 2:16 (ESV)

We move from rest, to faith and trust.

We return to the archway of trust, day by day and minute by minute. Our eyes turn back to Him, to rest in Him, every moment. Our remembrance of Him in us, our knowledge of His unrelenting presence, causes us to be aware that we live and move and have our being in Him (Acts 17:28).

He becomes more trustworthy to us as we see Him move, and then hold the testimony of His movements in our Hearts.

Returning to remember with Him, and engage, hook in, and be a partaker of all He does in our lives, brings us into a depth of relationship we never knew was possible.

Every vision, dream, and encounter, carries substance: food, drink, refreshing, instruction, strategy, wisdom, peace, joy. This is tangible life-giving fruit. Eat of the table He lays before you with absolute belief and trust in its truth and reality.

Now we move forward having been restored, and continuing to be restored.

The season is that of quick restoration, as we partake of revelation flowing from Heaven. The Lord truly becomes our rear guard, as He separates us from our past, and moves us through open doors into deeper revelation of Him, His word, and His ways.

Maturity and wisdom speak from a platform of authority given to the surrendered soul.

The carnal nature has been put to death, and now we walk as New Creations, a peculiar people, Ambassadors of The Kingdom (1 Peter 2:9, 2 Corinthians 5:11-21).

Our language is different as we allow each other the grace and space to grow in Christ.

Honouring Him within ourselves and each other, there is no longer a feeling of being threatened or put down in the presence of one walking in their calling.

We rejoice in Christ, us in Him, and Him in us, revelling in the wells of each one's experience, being refreshed in the company of the saints. We can partake of aspects of His nature, coming forth all around us, as each one shines with the glory and fullness of Christ within them.

We have become a table of spices as we share the revelation, the sweet honeycomb of His love, His empowering and His union with each other.

"…I have tasted and enjoyed my wine within you. I have tasted with pleasure my pure milk, my honeycomb, which you yield to me. I delight in gathering my sacred spice, all the fruits of my life I have gathered from within you, my paradise garden. Come, all my friends – feast upon my bride, all you revelers of my palace. Feast on her, my lovers! Drink and drink,and drink again…"

Song of Songs 5:1 (TPT)

Awake and Run

Awake and run, arise and run, with Spirit lips divine.

Speak the words within the wave, arise, rise up and shine.

The language new, the people ready to receive the holy grace

The wave and ripples coming forth, from gazing at His face.

"Rise up and listen, and run boldly in the new

I'll do a new thing, and this I will tell to you.

It's time to move, it's time to shake, and go through heaven's doors

It's time to release, step on up, and walk into the more."

Lord, lead me, guide me through open space, into my Land of promise

You know the way to Heaven's Gate, come on, and lead me on it.

"Rest and sit, and make the plans, of all I've said before,

Believe that now it's time to move, to walk through open doors."

All hell will try to stop us, so write the vision, make it plain,

For the promised land is waiting on us, to start to rule and reign.

"The new is that the time has come to MOVE in joy and RUN

The new is that it's breakthrough time - see the face of my true Son.

The new is that the promises, have now all come to pass

The miraculous is springing forth, creation's reign now past.

The Sons of God are rising, to take their rightful place

The new is now creation bows, and gazes on My face.

So, as you've said, now make it plain, for what I've said will start

The need is for others to read the plan, so RUN, and GO, and FAST.

Put it right before your face, words of truth and destination.

Arise and shine your light has come, draw in all the nations.

Tell them that the time has come, to rise and run and go

Tell them that the Bridegrooms coming and it's time to be on show

It's time to strap on boots of peace, the Shield of Faith's been hewn

It's time to pick up sceptres, and signet rings been given

Take the sword and run with speed, the race that you are in now

The promises and open doors, go to and through and enter now.

You've stayed the course, and pushed on through, overcomers are what you are

The new is waiting through Heavens' Gate, come let's Go – let's start.

To heal with words of truth and love, to smile and love and listen.

Don't think of all you have to do – be My hands and vision."

Take the time, and settle back into His loving mercy.

The simple gospel truth of wholeness – going down in history.

The great revival has begun - be activated - join The Son.

Twenty

Walking in Two Worlds with Presence

In the heart of Jesus, you are cherished and trusted.

In His heart, all you were created to *be* pales into insignificance as you sit in the secret chamber of delicious love, surrounded in such peace that you want to live there. It is from the heart of The King, that you now carry substance.

You have absorbed His life, His light, His essence. You cannot go from there unchanged, or without anointing to affect those around your life. From the place of His heart you carry Presence. You carry Majesty. You carry perspective.

The perspective of a King. Everything you look at, you will see through the eyes of love and certainty of victory. Circumstances will not shift you, but you will be a shifter of circumstances even as you walk into difficult situations, instilled with confidence.

You are a carrier of the light, a mover of mountains and a giant-slayer, just by spending time with the giver of life, breathing His substance, and being transformed by the power of His Word.

You become a carrier of Presence.

True humility is knowing who you are. Gently walking in the revelation of that truth causes the Love of Jesus to permeate the atmosphere. Whether you are a joy-carrier, an intercessor, a teacher, or a prophet, love pours forth like living waters.

Others are drawn into the Presence of Christ and ignited, as the fire of Christ in you ignites Holy fire inside of them.

We have the privilege and honour of leading, in humility, those who are hungry and thirsty.

As we walk in two worlds, being part of this one but not of it, the substance of His presence remains on us. It sticks to us like honey to our fingers.

With a word, an impartation of Heaven comes.

Because we gazed into His face and beheld His glory, He will woo others through us into His secret chamber, causing them also to release the old, stale ways of works and format, for the intimacy and knowledge of His heart.

He will encounter us in a place of rest, where we lie down and become a partaker of the sweetness of His presence, His life, His love. Resting, we leave behind the heavy-laden burdens of slavery and bondage, coming into the sweet honey of Bridal intimacy.

We enter under a banner of rest and love. His Holy place. His Heart.

Now we come to resurrection life.

All the pain of hope deferred has been anointed within the healing honey of His presence, and we walk in a deeper revelation of LIFE in Christ.

We begin to understand our seat and destiny of co-reigning with Christ, seated in Heavenly places in Him. We speak healing miracles into the sick. From a place of authority we declare resurrection into the places of death which should be living: healing lands, governments, peoples and nations.

As we take our seats of government in the Heavens, atmospheres open up to our spiritual eyes. We push back the darkness with the light and life of Christ, by showing up in the realm of the spirit to release decrees that change circumstances.

From here we have risen, and shine for our light has come, and the glory of the Lord is risen upon us (Isaiah 60:1-5). Nations will come to the brightness of our rising as we begin to declare and decree miracles, signs and wonders coming forth in greater degrees of power and number.

Our countenance and manner changes. We attract people like moths to a flame as we walk in the resurrection power of our Holy God.

You have been found trustworthy in the secret place, in the leaning upon and moving out of His heart. Now a sceptre is passed into your hands to govern with the wisdom and compassion of Christ, which is only given by the power of His Spirit.

> "My old identity has been co-crucified with Messiah and no longer lives; for the nails of his cross crucified me with him. And now the essence of this new life is no longer mine, for the Anointed One lives his life through me – we live in union as one! My new life is empowered by the faith of the Son of God who loves me so much that he gave himself for me, and dispenses his life into mine!"
>
> Galatians 2:20 (TPT)

I am a temple of Holy Spirit, and as revelation of this is imparted into my spirit man, the core of my soul is transformed into His likeness.

Christ in me now assures me that in all I do, victory is sure, no matter what it looks like in the natural.

I have had 2 experiences which have profoundly impacted how I see the authority I walk in as a new creation in Christ:

In 2019 I went to Israel. We had left Jerusalem and stopped in Galilee for two nights. On the final morning before we were to return to Tel Aviv and fly out, I was walking with Holy Spirit, with a very open, soft heart, just absorbing the land.

I was sorrowful to be leaving and deeply grateful for the opportunity I'd had in being there. As this gratefulness flooded my entire being, it seemed my heart physically expanded within me as I was looking at a mountain in the distance.

As I worshiped, and gazed upon the mountain, it was as if the whole earth moved. The mountain moved into my heart. I felt it shift physically, and saw it also. Since that time, I have carried Galilee, like it is my homeland of New Zealand. It is a part of me.

This was my first experience of our living Earth.

In a more recent event, I was in New Zealand, walking again, a couple of days before I left to return home to Australia.

I was feeling the same. A deep sorrow at leaving the land and this time my family also.

I went for a walk down to a bridge that is a driveway to three private properties further on. It is surrounded by mountains and bushland.

The sorrow became so deep in me, like an intercession, and I prayed for Yahweh to help me cope with this, as I couldn't see how I could function back home in Australia, in this deeply sad state.

 Before the prayer had left me, I began to worship, overcome by the beauty that surrounded me, in awe of the majesty of this creation. Holy Spirit was flowing from me as I began to call forth the mountains to praise the Lord. I called out with great passion for the trees to clap their hands, and for the rocks to cry out in worship.

I had never prayed like that before, so passionate with gratefulness and as the sorrow left, a deep sense of Majesty engulfed me: The Earth's majesty, Christ's majesty and that of my own and fellow saints, which is still in the process of being revealed and understood.

I could see, and feel all of creation, waking up from its slumbering state and rejoicing at the manifestation of a son. It really was majestic.

I stayed for quite some time, dancing with Jesus on the bridge, not caring too much if anyone was watching, just overcome in worship.

Both occasions were driven by heartfelt sorrow at leaving a land.

Having returned home to Australia, I was then led into a vision which was quite astounding:

Holy Spirit took me into a long room, with desks and typewriters on one side and a large bay window with glass to the ceiling on the other. It was a very old-looking room, with an 18th century look about it. Coming through the window was a very bright light.

I must say, I was a bit apprehensive to look out. I understood in my spirit man, this was a room where I would receive revelation and sight. Holy Spirit, in the form of Revelation, was standing with me.

When I looked out the window, I saw myself worshiping on the bridge. As I did, Holy Spirit said to me, "I want to show you what happened here, in The Kingdom, when you did that."

I could see I was looking down from the window of Revelation, down onto myself on the bridge. I could see myself on the bridge, and between me, in the Revelation room, and me on the bridge, was a portal into Heaven. There were many witnesses gathered around the edge of the portal, watching. Angels and the greater cloud.

As I was calling forth the mountains to praise the Lord, and the trees to clap their hands, and for the rocks to cry out, those gathered around the portal in Heaven fell to their knees weeping, at the manifestation of The Son in me and at what God is about to do.

There was a ripping in Heaven of a veil, and it seemed the edges of the portal were torn open on one side, and on the other side, over the bridge, and the river. The Earth collided with Heaven. It was real and intense.

I believe it has now become what some would term as 'a thin place', an anchor point of Heaven, as His Kingdom has come on Earth. Somewhere that The Kingdom of God is accessed with less degree of resistance by the prince of the power of the air.

There was a sense of rocking, and locking on.

A few days earlier I had a revelation, while in conversation with my sister, of what Heaven and Earth coming together actually looks like.

I saw the mountains and valleys of the Earth, and around the edges of the Earth I saw the mountains and valleys of Heaven – as if a reflection.

These two worlds are fitting together like a jigsaw, but there are mountains on Earth where there shouldn't be. I think of the areas of finance, education, and media, where the enemy has deep strongholds. I am sure there are many you could think of also. These mountains on Earth that are not in alignment with The Kingdom are holding back The Kingdom. But they are being ground down, shuddering and breaking up under the pressure of God's Kingdom coming.

They are breaking, under a revealing of all things that are hidden in the darkness coming into the light, as saints become aware of, and carry their authority into the dark places, releasing the light, with ease.

There is immense pressure on Earth, even physically, as the bringing down of the mountains and raising up of the valleys happens, as this alignment, which is inevitable, begins to manifest.

As we, The Sons, The Bride, walk in our rightful authority, even calling forth the Earth to praise Him, Heaven takes up residence on Earth. Everything that has breath Praises Him, Yahweh.

Oh my!

Our whole experience of Christianity is being shifted by The King.

Vision – A New Portal Opened

I saw a brand-new portal, with a membrane around the edges, recently broken. There is a waterfall flowing down upon the Earth, which is fresh and green.

As a Baptism from death to life, completely and freely, we move into this new realm of existence, in Purity, Holiness, Truth, Honesty and Integrity.

Jesus spoke to me saying:

"Nurture the newness of life in the Spirit. Know that I am accomplishing my purposes. Speak life in Holiness, into the

new Earth and into the atmosphere that is as a garden prepared for seed.

You speak the words of resurrection life and restoration flows from My Throne as we talk of what you see in Heaven. You speak it out, to me, and into the atmosphere, and you will see a manifestation of My Glory.

My Word is power and life. My word creates. Speak to me about My Words, and I will speak to you about creation.

Watch me change your personal world.

Speak life, and watch me change your Nation.

Words of life are cultivating your atmosphere."

We are His shining ones, a peculiar people, shining the light of Christ with His strength and power.

The Kingdom realm travels with us, as we go into all the world with the light of the Gospel, and the power of Resurrection Life of the Holy Spirit.

You carry the atmosphere that causes people to breathe.

You are the access point of God into the Earth.

You are the open portal.

You carry the sweetness of His presence.

You carry Christ to the world.

We are turned inside out and the one we carry within becomes visible to the world. The weighty glory of revelation from the secret place streams forth, and manifests as light.

Jesus spoke to me in regards to the shifts and changes happening swiftly around us:

"Though things may look the same in circumstance, the spirit realm is changed and you move forward now with victory and strength that has been foreign to you in the past.

Now you begin to carry My Government, as I release in you greater authority, from the place of intimacy.

You are a movement, without false humility or pride, which is exactly how Heaven sees you.

You are a building a structure of many rooms, within which are my hidden treasures.

"You are a city of grace with power. Explosive power to shift and change and move in the heavens.

You are filled with my fullness. Let it build within and push it out.

You walk out of My heart, with Presence.

You shift atmospheres when you walk in the room, by the power of Holy Spirit and the sound released when you speak."

And so, we decree, looking at our King, in oneness with Him, speaking back to Him what He is saying in regards to any given situation.

We agree with His word, crafting prayers and decrees, not from a place of fear, striving, or pride, out of a formulated plan or structure, but from the secret place, knowing His plans, His truth, and His way.

We war with a majestic authority, with the confidence and boldness of one with the signet ring of The Lord, having been dipped in the Blood of Mercy, Truth, and Wisdom.

In quietness and confidence, we have peace. Strength exudes from our inner man.

The Sword of Truth is wielded with intention and accuracy as we listen to His instruction, heed His word and remain in the peace and love of his strong tower.

The light of His presence shines forth from us as we walk out into the world, infused with the indwelling power of His Spirit in our inner being (Eph 3:16).

Joy is our portion and our cup, as we are constantly aware of who walks within.

The Bride is rising up.

Twenty One

To Be Continued...

Continue to press in.

Continue to always make your relationship with Christ your priority. If you find yourself slipping, beginning to focus on worldly issues, put your blinkers on again, and re-settle yourself back into His loving arms.

He is kind, gracious, and supremely in love with you and me.

This is the height of our walk with Yahweh.

The veil was torn.

We are one.

"Things never discovered or heard of before, things beyond our ability to imagine- these are the many things God has in store for all His lovers.

But God now unveils these profound realities to us by the Spirit. Yes, he has revealed to us his inmost heart and deepest mysteries through the Holy Spirit, who constantly explores all things. After all, who can really see into a person's heart and know his hidden impulses except for that person's spirit? So it is with God. His thoughts and secrets are only fully understood by his Spirit, the Spirit of God.

For we did not receive the spirit of this world system but the Spirit of God, so that we might come to understand and experience all that grace has lavished upon us. And we articulate these realities with words imparted to us by the Spirit and not with words taught by human wisdom. We join together Spirit-revealed truths and Spirit-revealed words. Someone living on an entirely human level rejects the revelations of God's Spirit, for they make no sense to him. He can't understand the revelations of the Spirit because they are only discovered by the illumination of the Spirit. Those who live in the Spirit are able to carefully evaluate all things, and they are subject to the scrutiny of no one but God. For who has ever intimately known the mind of the Lord Yahweh well enough to become his counsellor?

CHRIST HAS, AND WE POSSESS CHRIST'S PERCEPTIONS!!!

1 Corinthians 2:9-16 (TPT)

IT'S ONLY THE BEGINNING.

About the Author

Jacqueline Taylor

Jacqueline is a prophetic minister whose desire is to shift old mind sets of any separateness between us and God and helping others to see their union and the potential they have, with Christ. Through words of prophesy and insight she has encouraged many to hope for greater things, as she ignites believers into a passion and depth of love for Jesus, that they can be transformed by the power of Holy Spirit and the love of Abba, Father.

Jacqueline is the founder of Honeyheart Connections, a ministry dedicated to reconnecting the hearts of God's people into union with Him and with one another.

Her second publication will be an interactive journal dedicated to deepening the bonds of relationship between mothers and daughters, that will be fun, profound, and simple to use.

Jacqueline was born again in Griffith, NSW, Australia, at the age of 28, and has been walking intimately with

Jesus, in visions and experience over that time. She has served as an Assistant Pastor, and leader, and now operates an itinerant ministry south of Perth, in Western Australia, where she lives with her husband, Rod, their dog, Pepper, rabbit Cloud, and fish Pykel and Fisher. She has 2 children and 6 grandchildren (so far ☺).

Design by Aerial View Studio
Amy Webb

Honeyheart Connections

At Rest - Connected -
Empowered

Design by Aerial Studio
Amy Webb

Printed in Great Britain
by Amazon

26515016R00096